PICTURE BOOK OF
WILDLIFE
ANIMALS

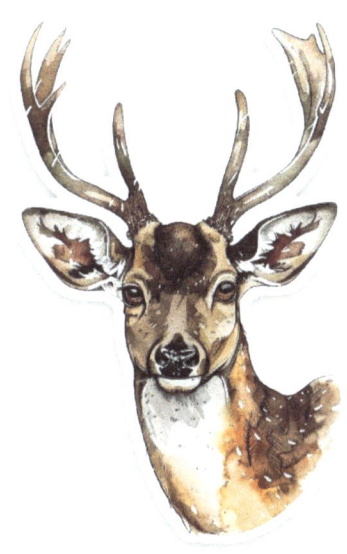

...By...

Ella Caldwell

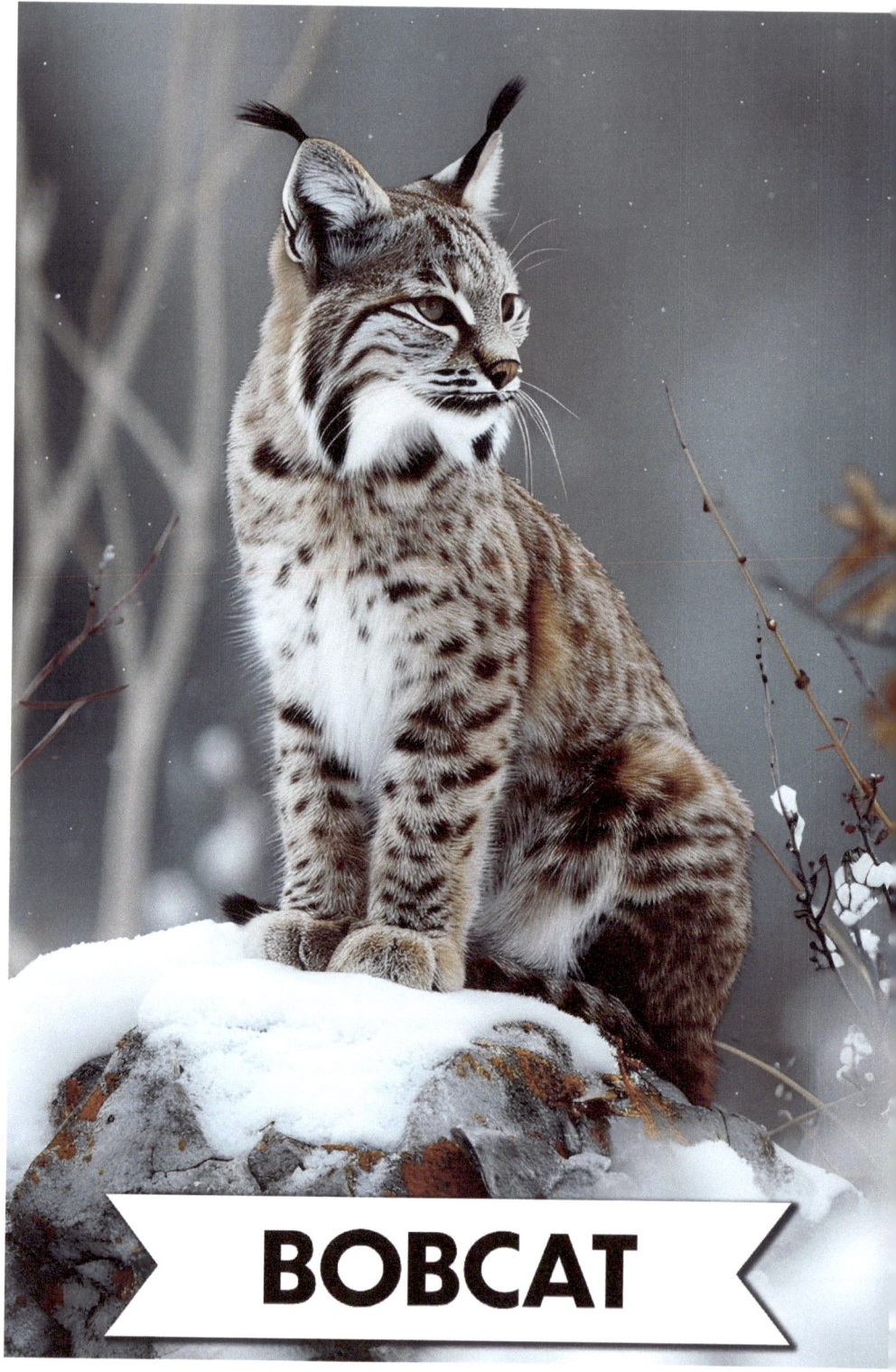

BOBCAT

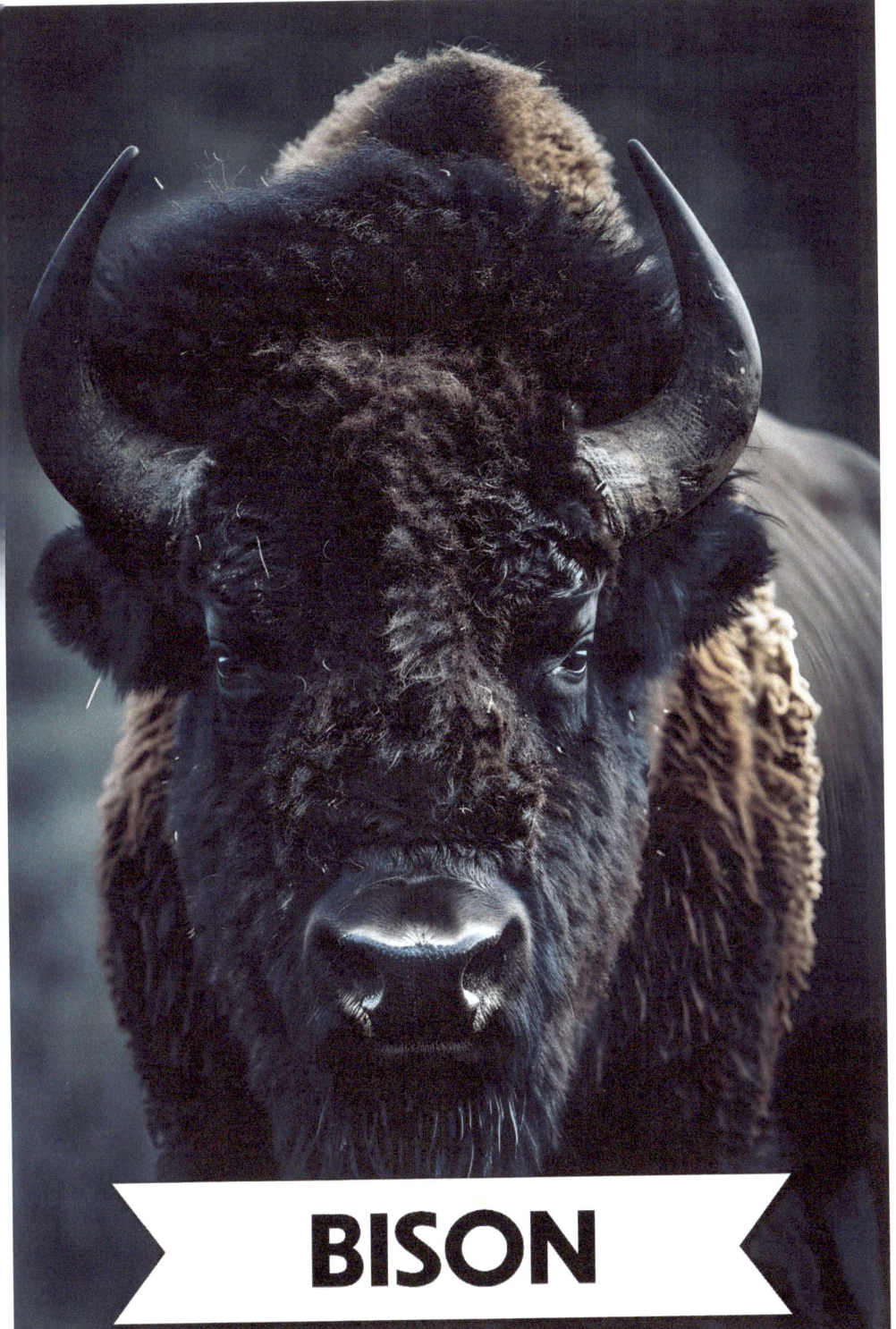

BISON

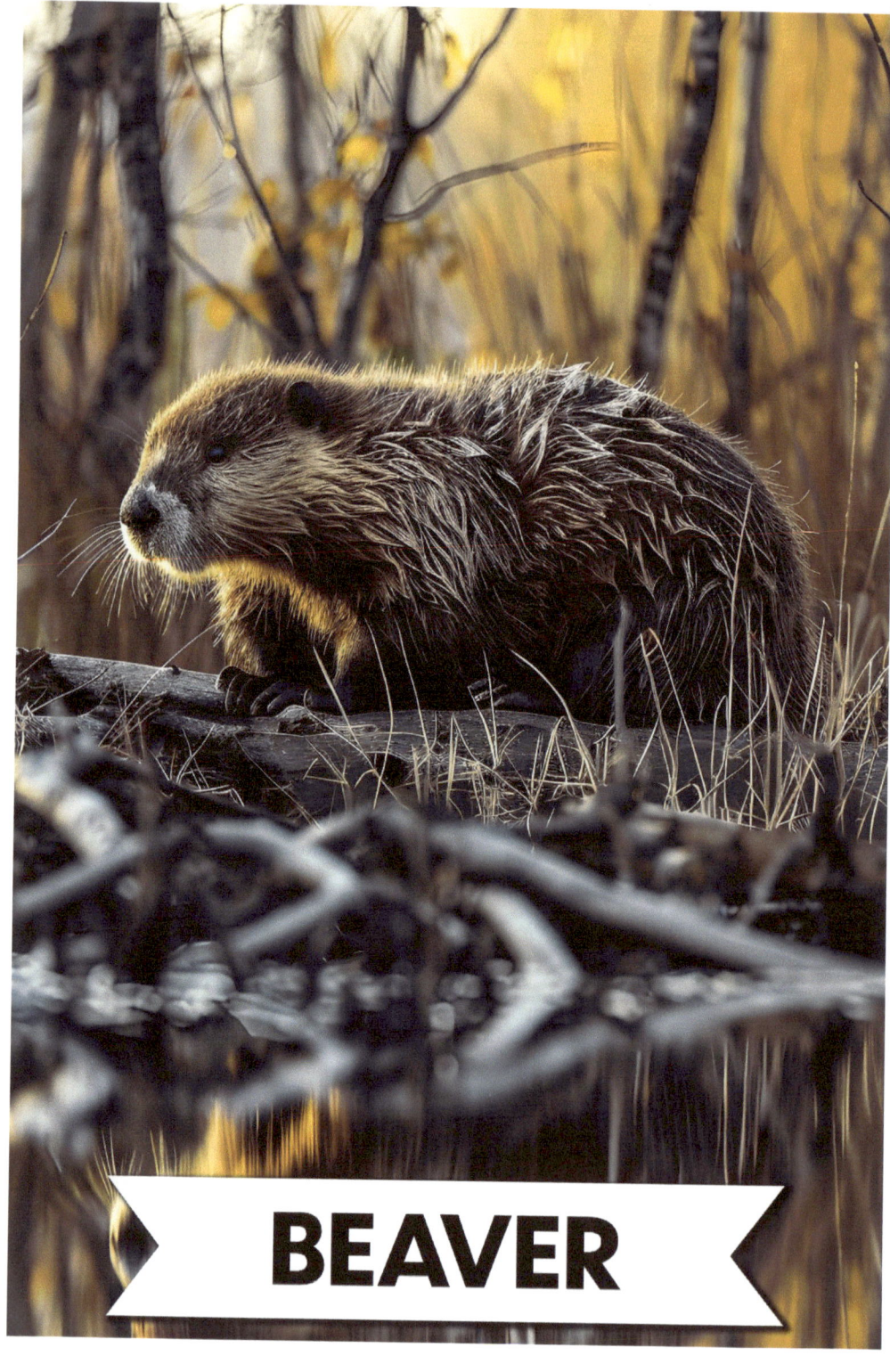

BEAVER

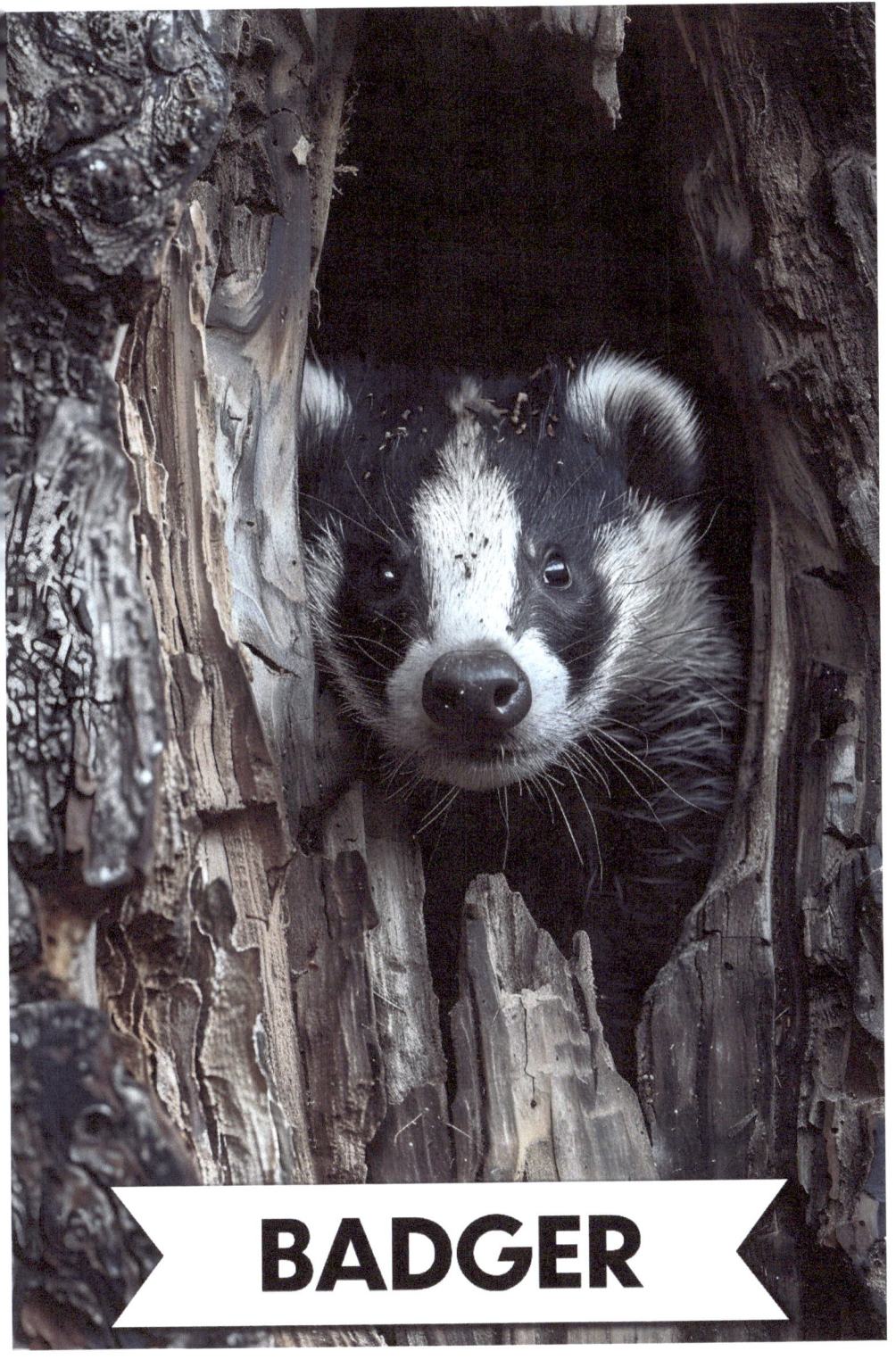

BADGER

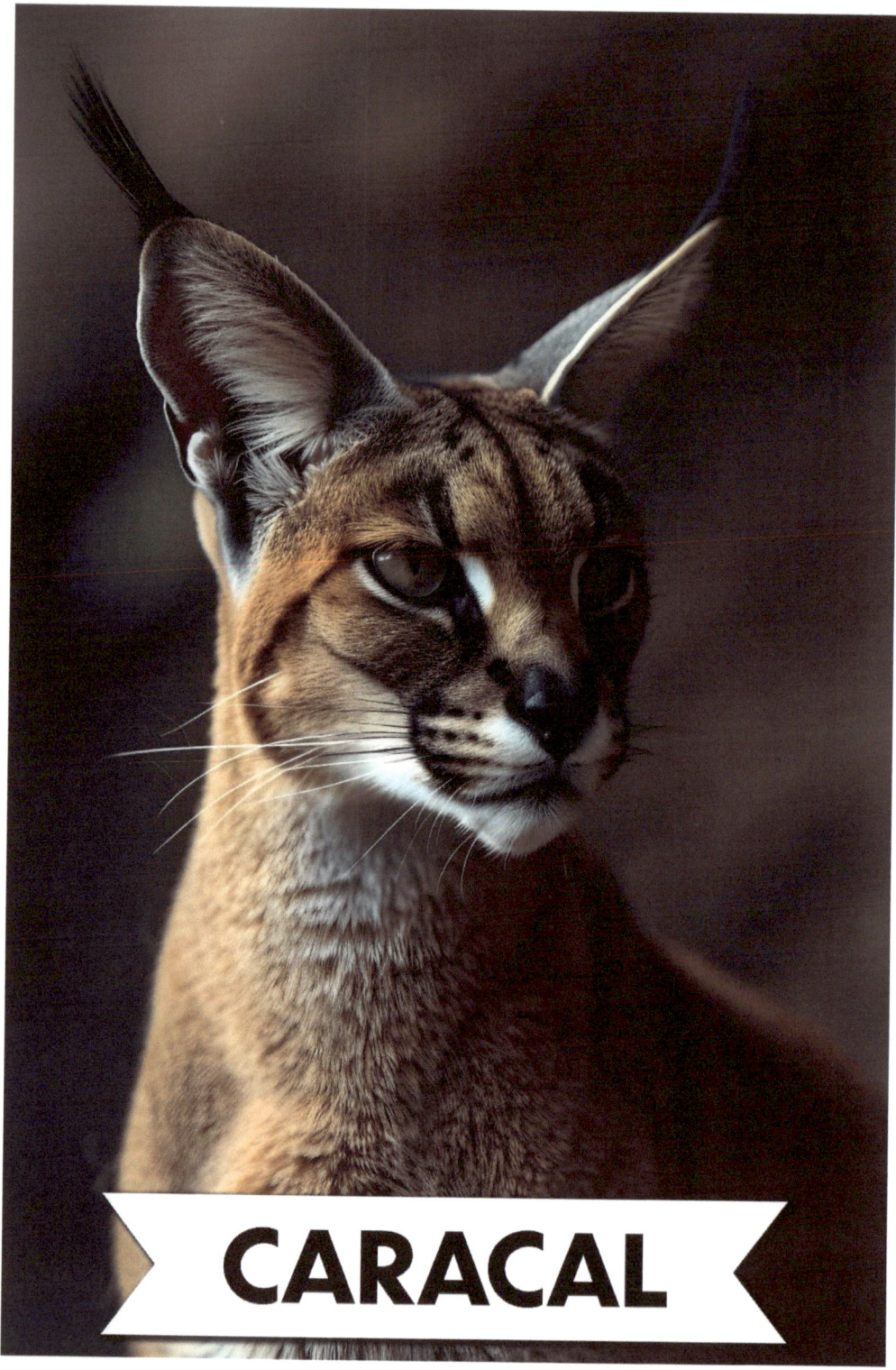

CARACAL

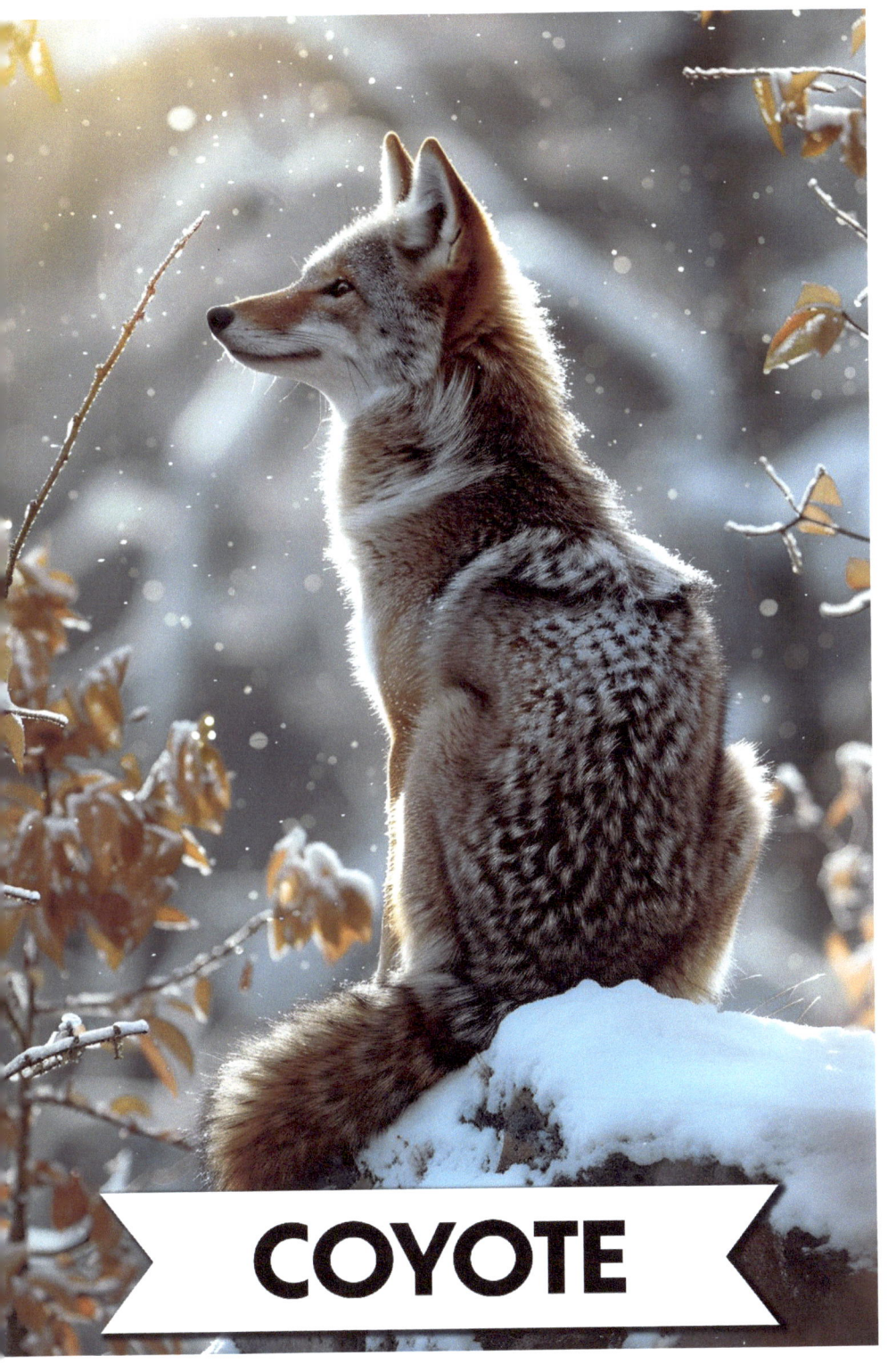

COYOTE

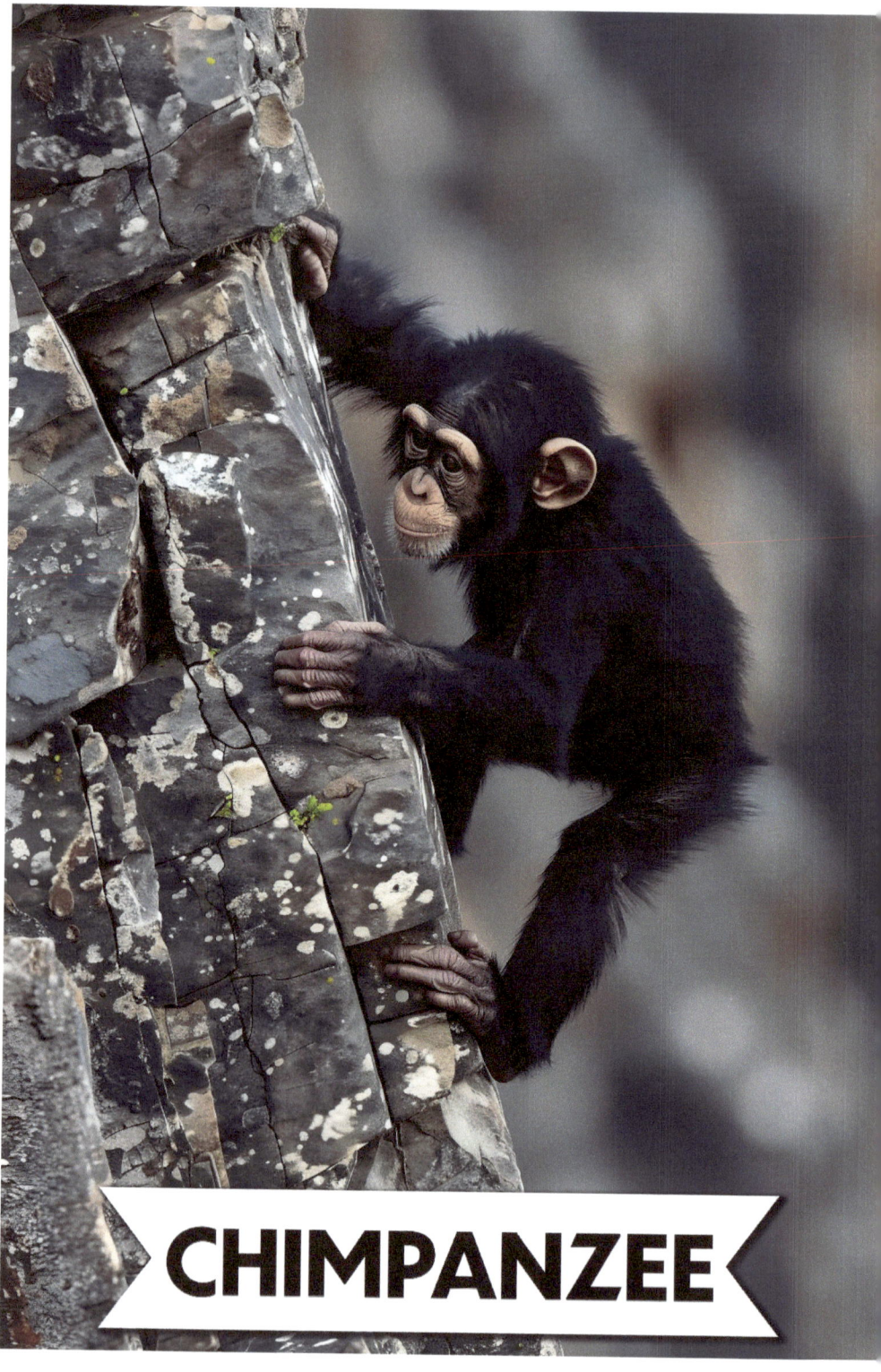

CHIMPANZEE

CHEETAH

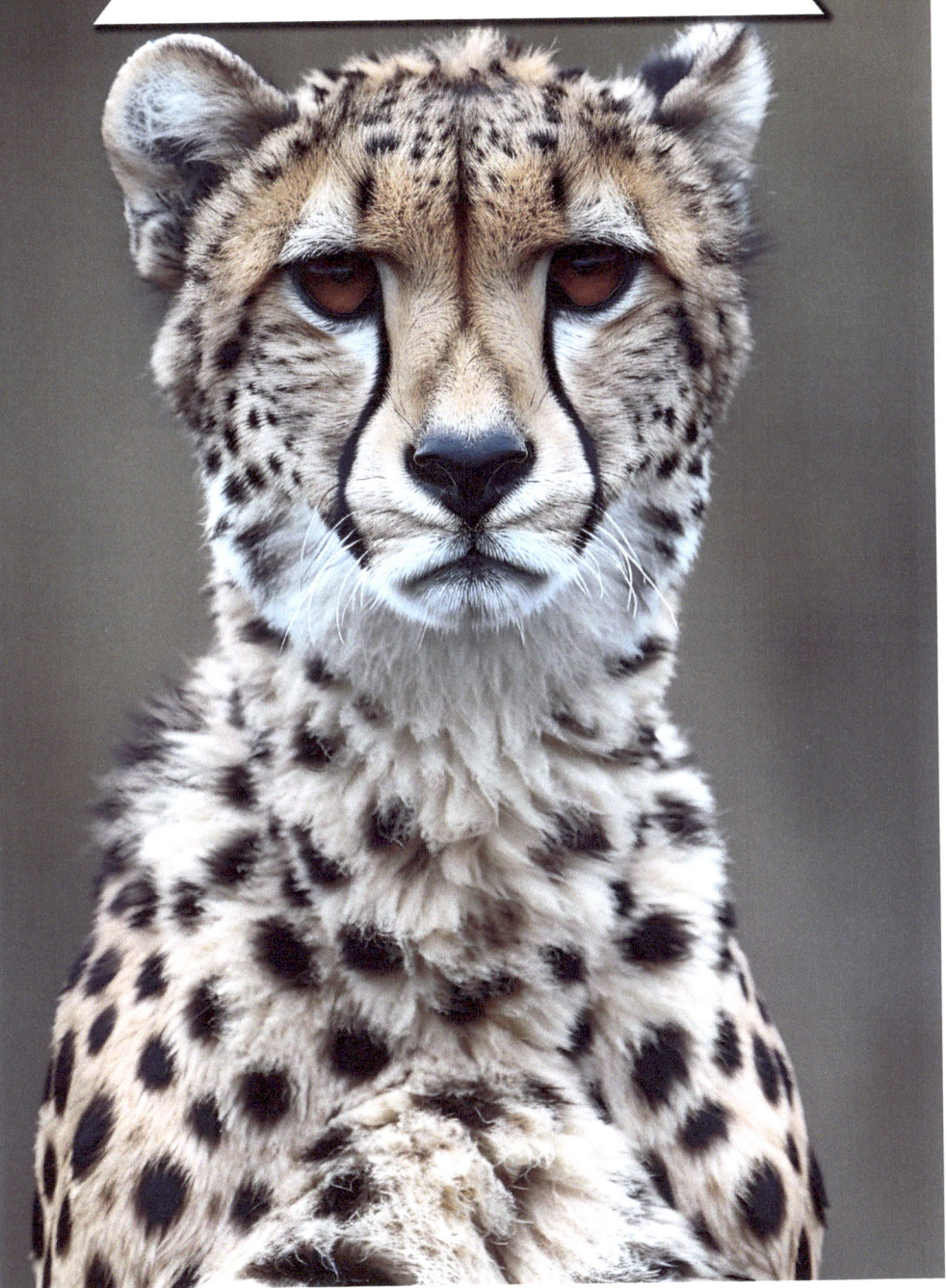

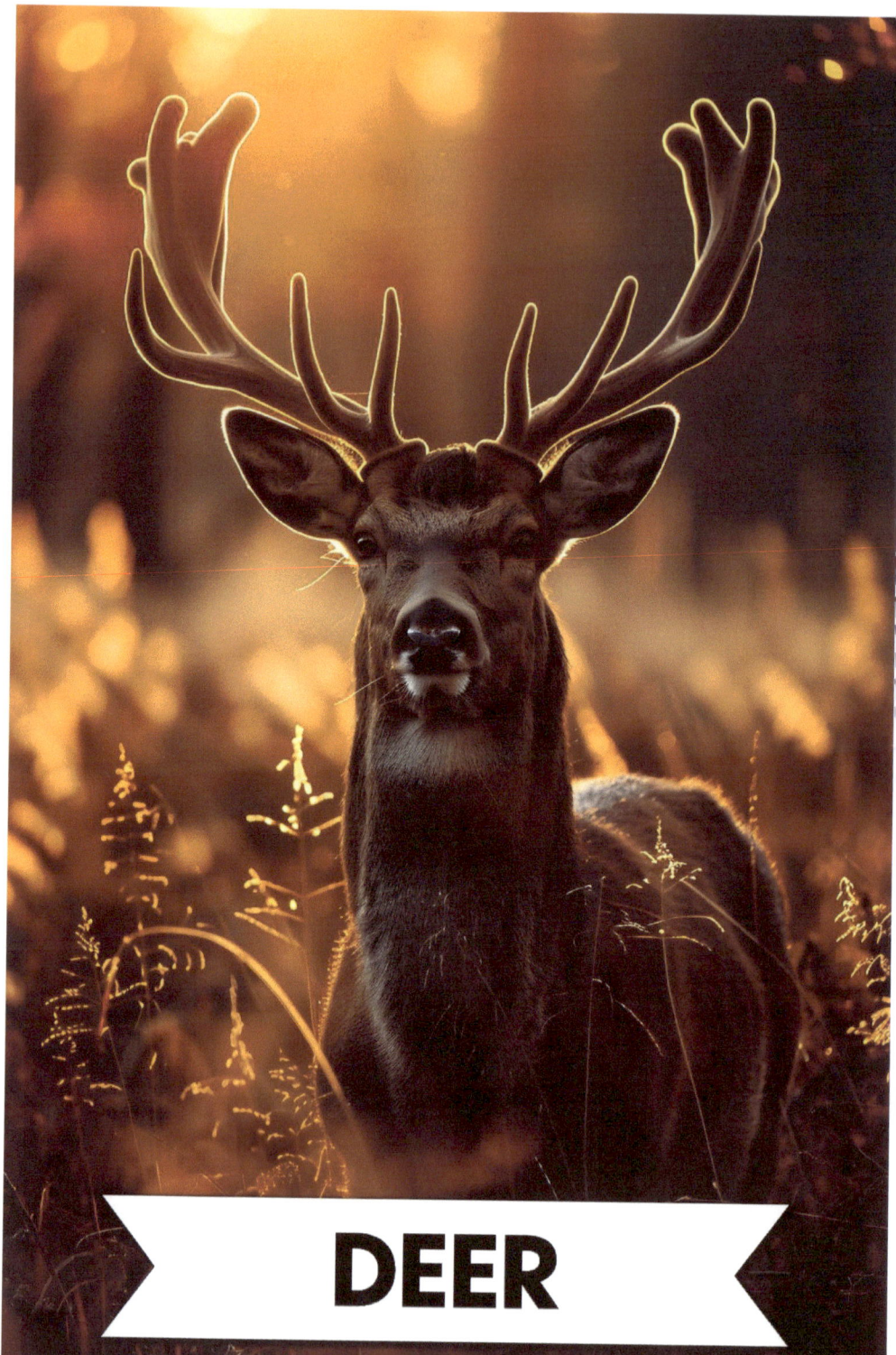

DEER

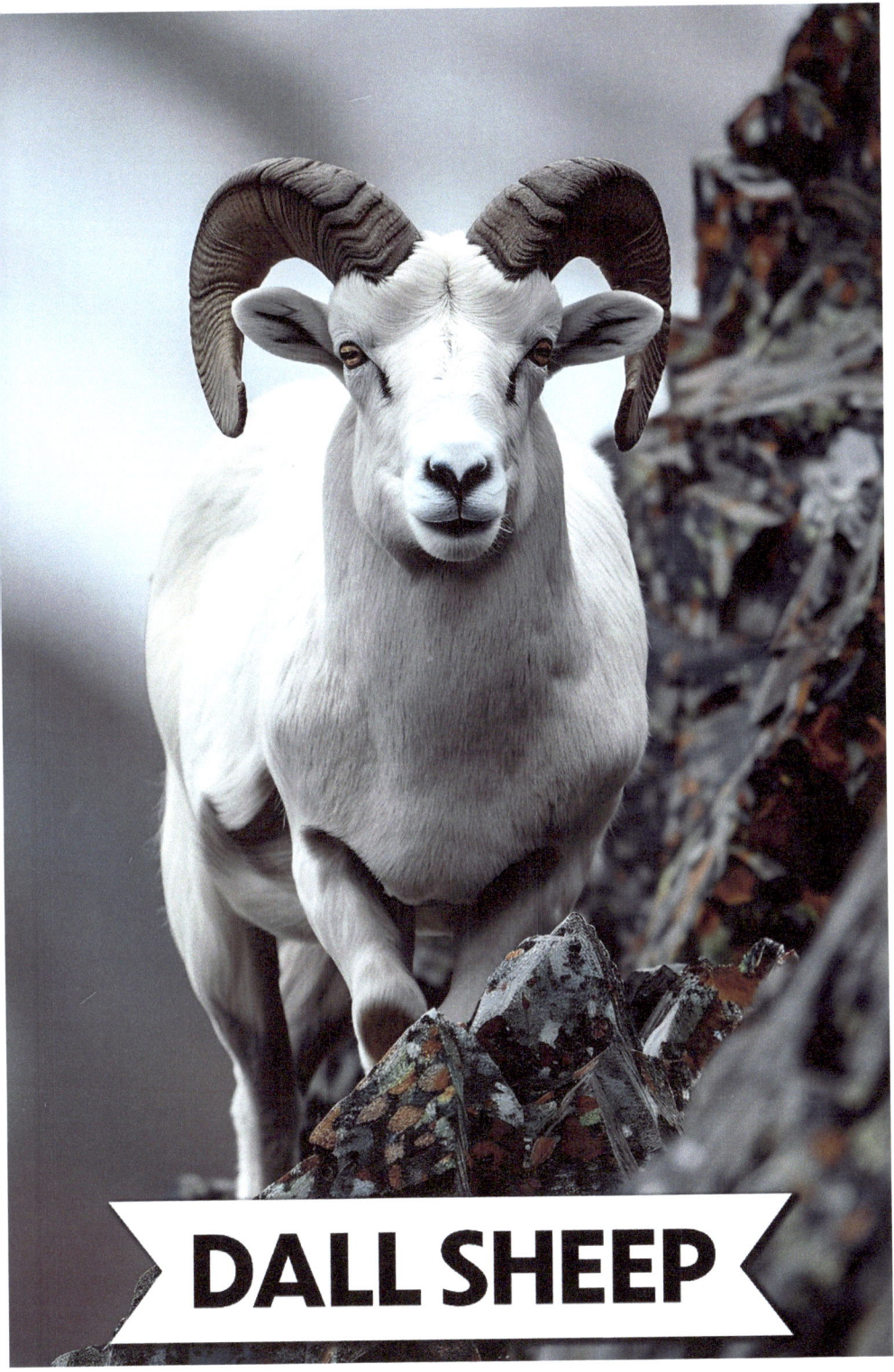

DALL SHEEP

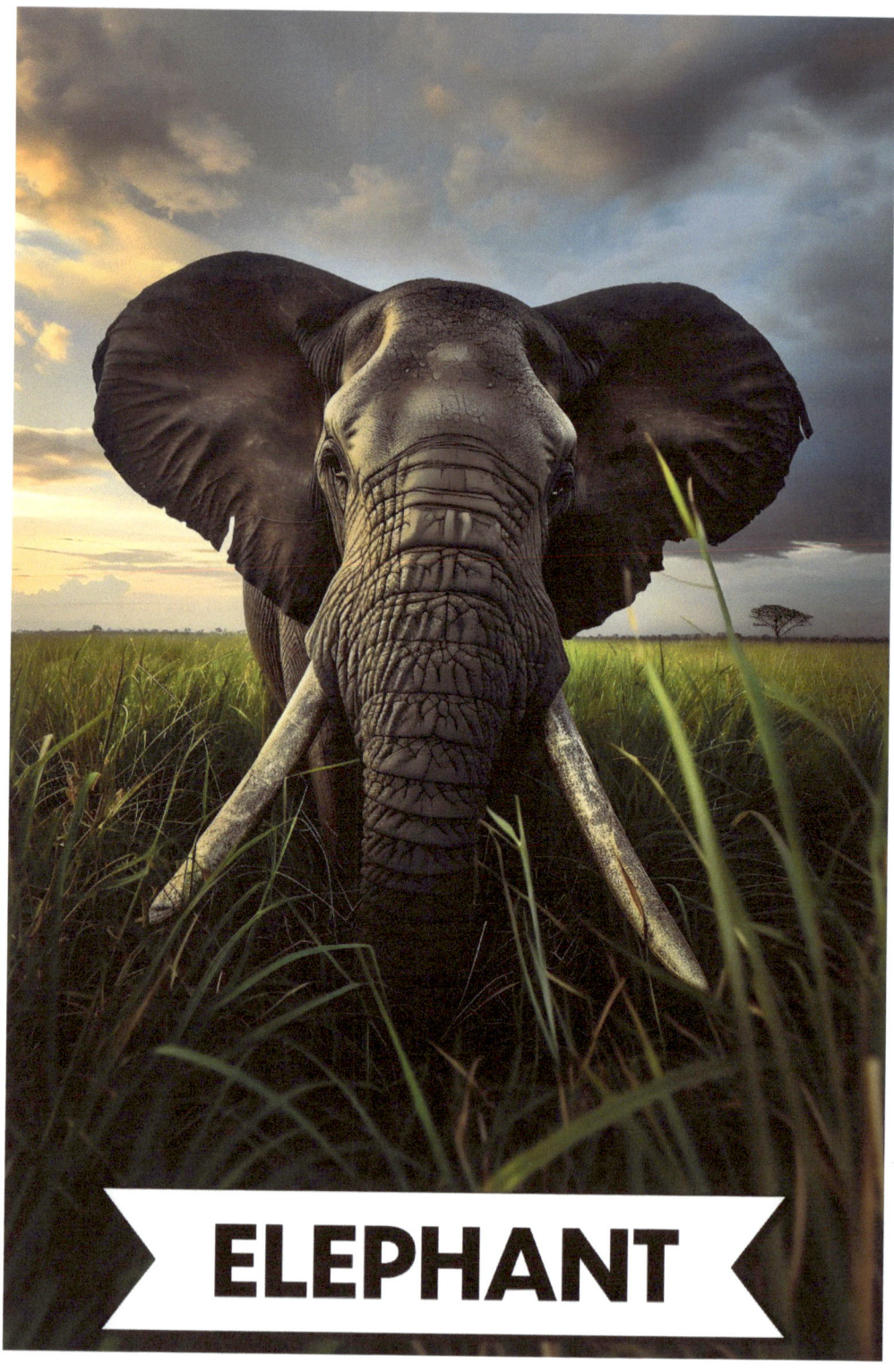

ELEPHANT

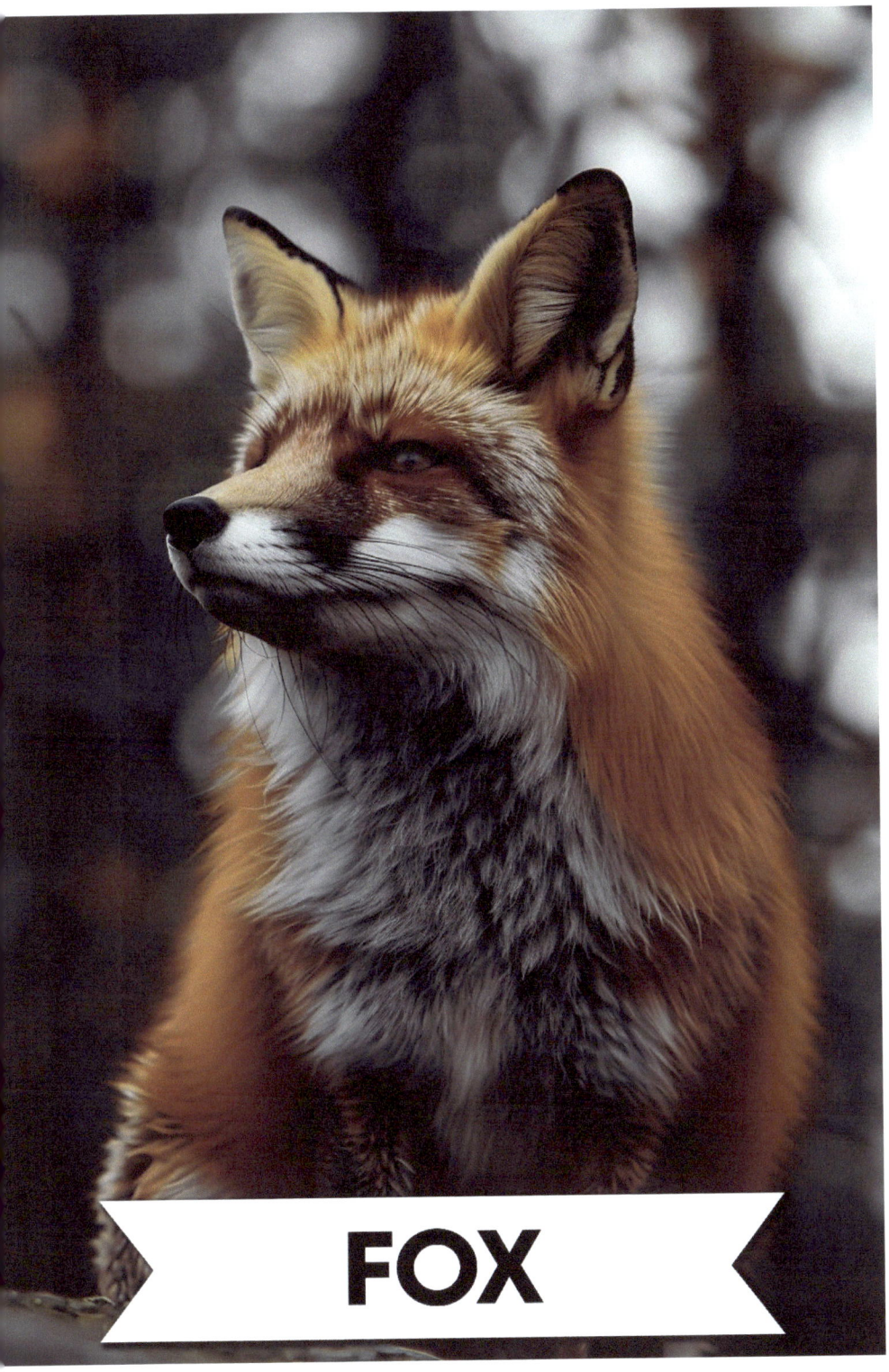

FOX

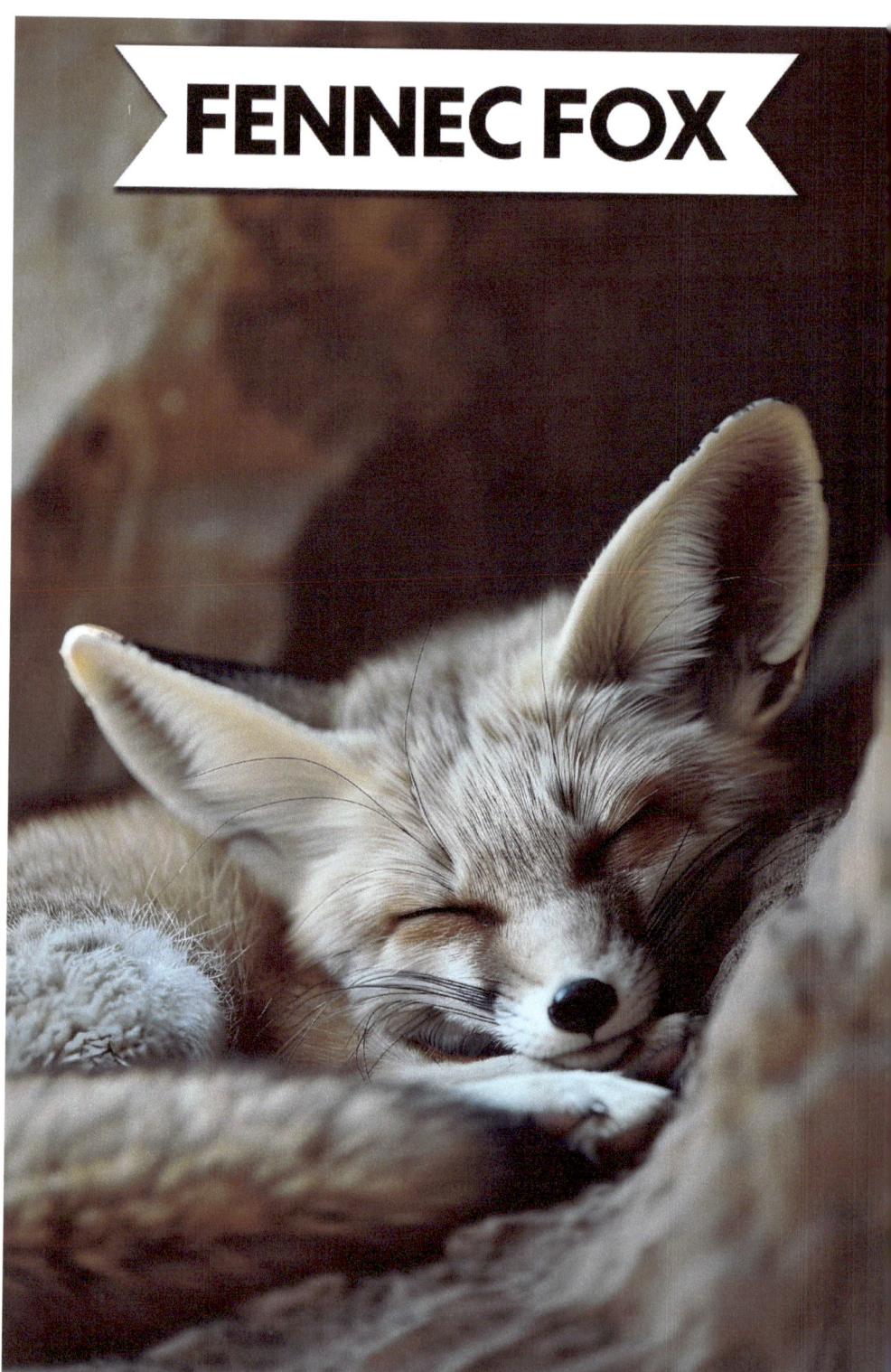

FENNEC FOX

GRIZZLY BEAR

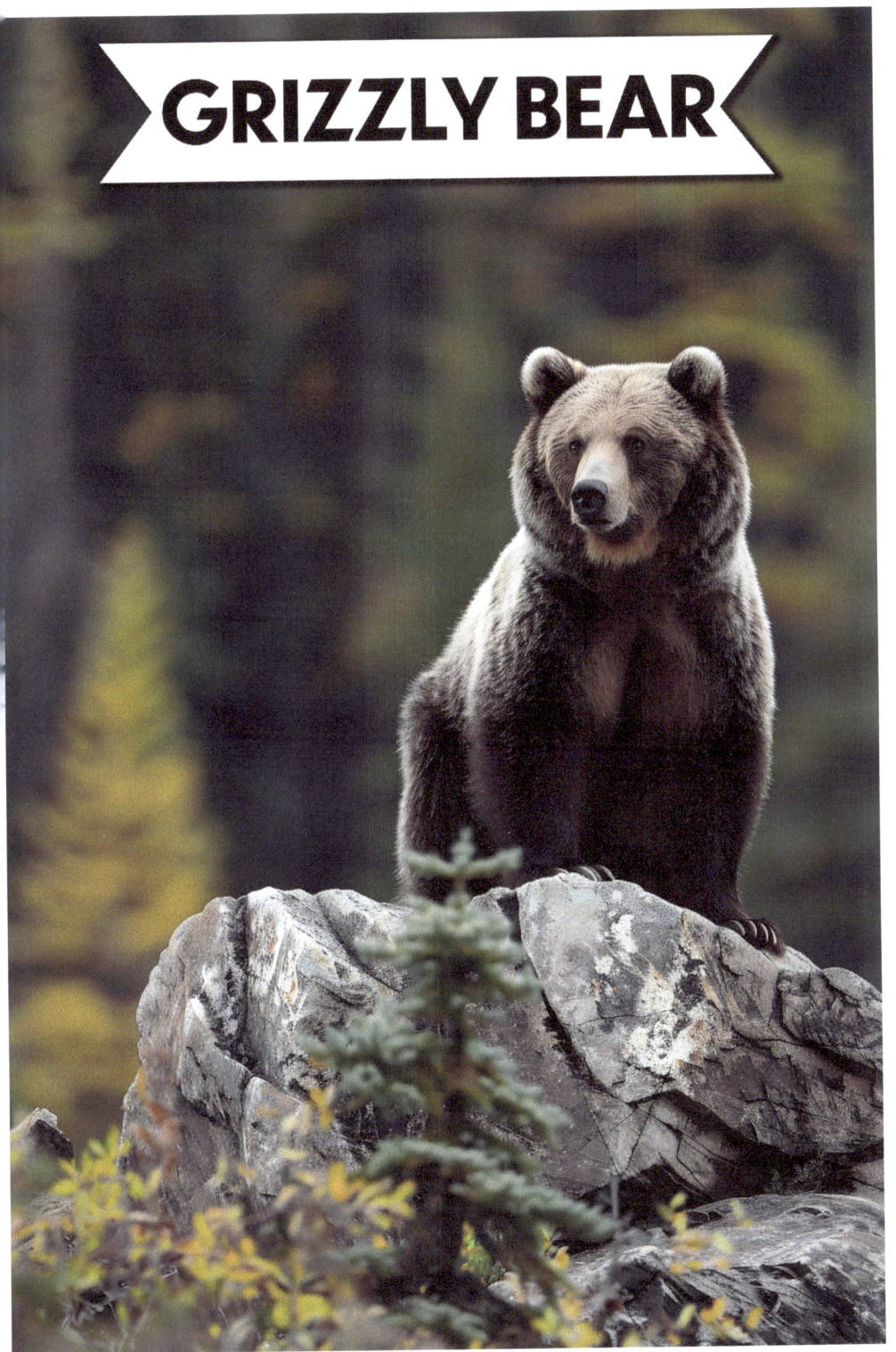

GORILLA

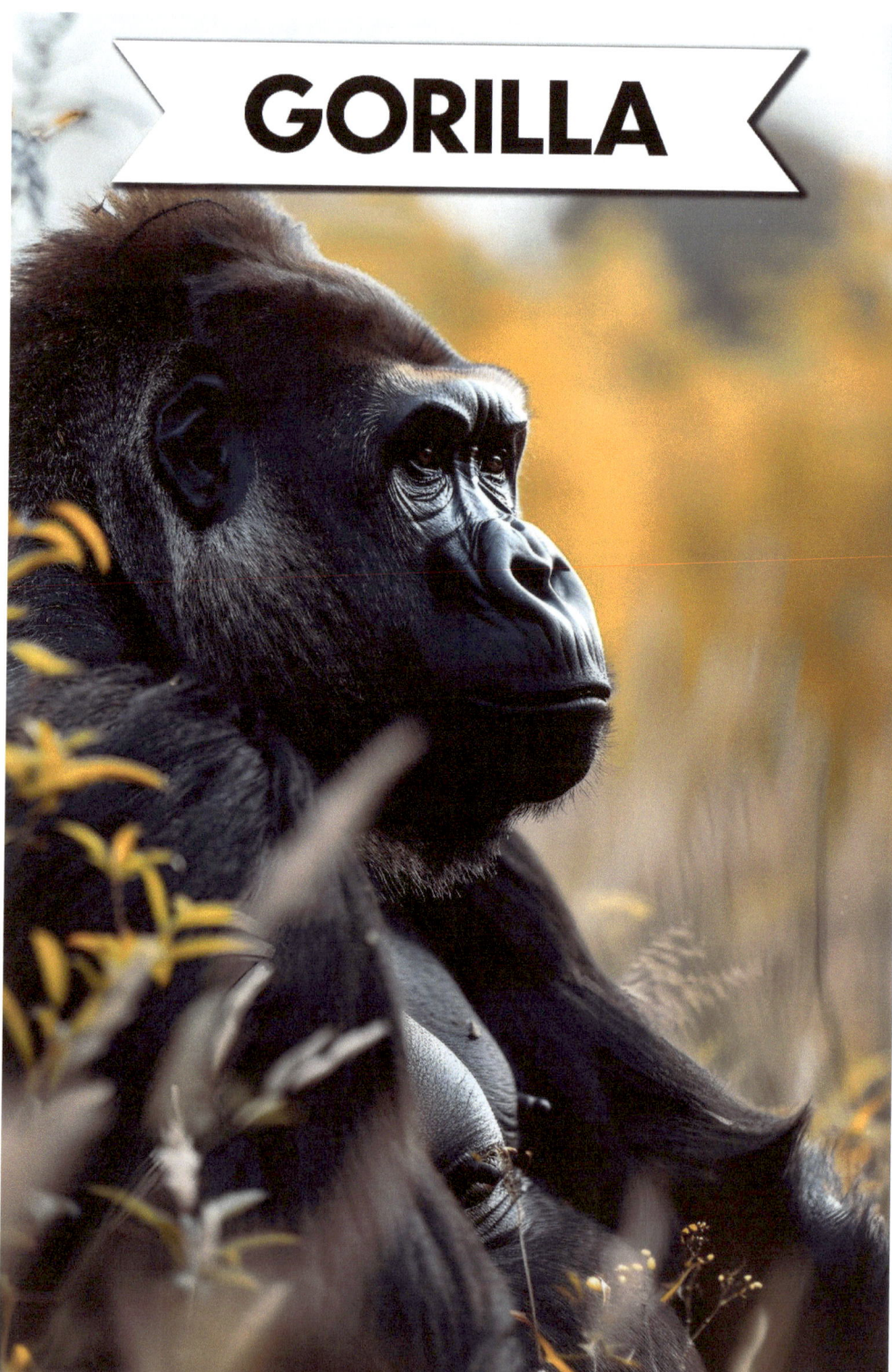

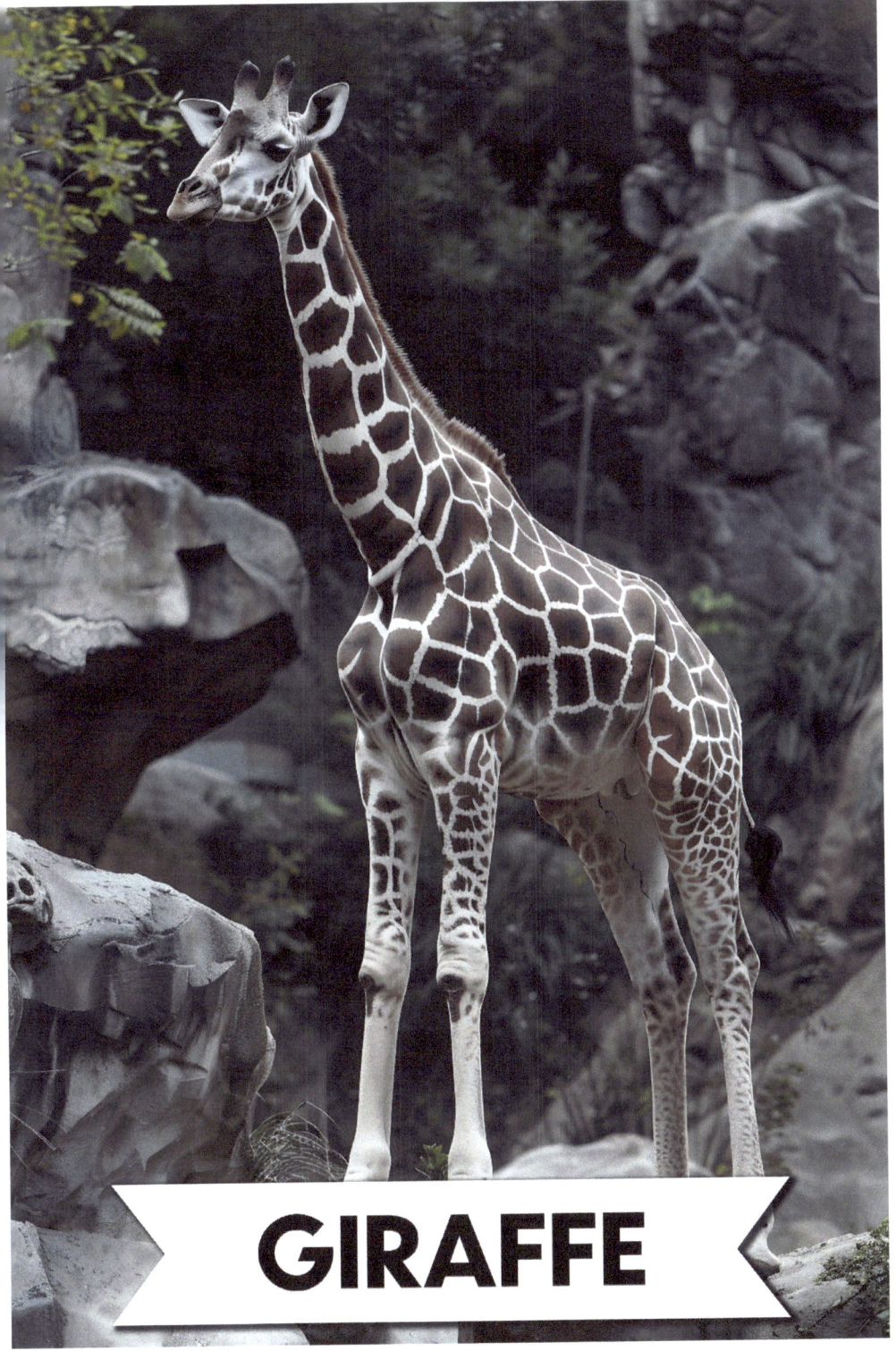

GIRAFFE

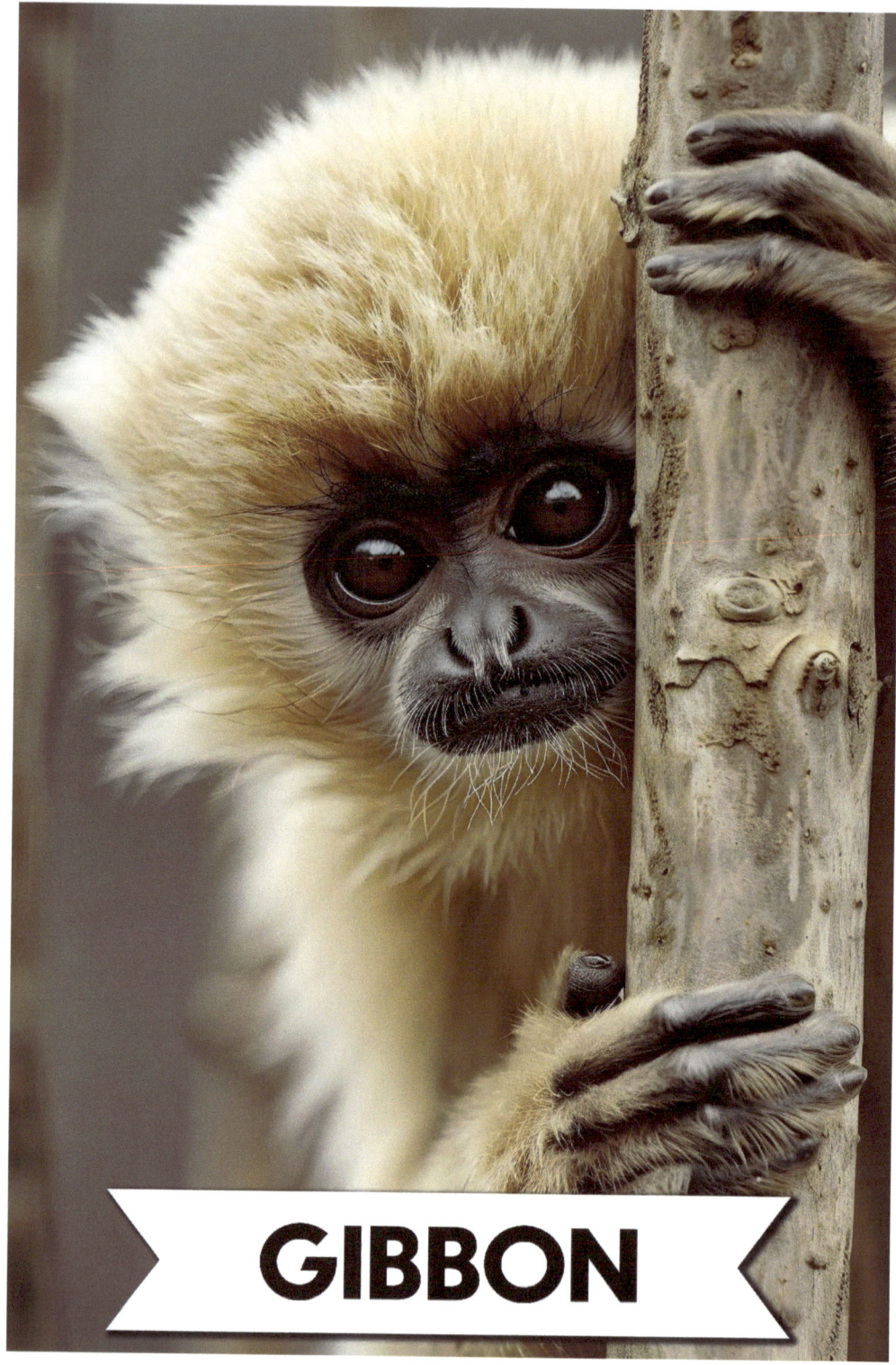

GIBBON

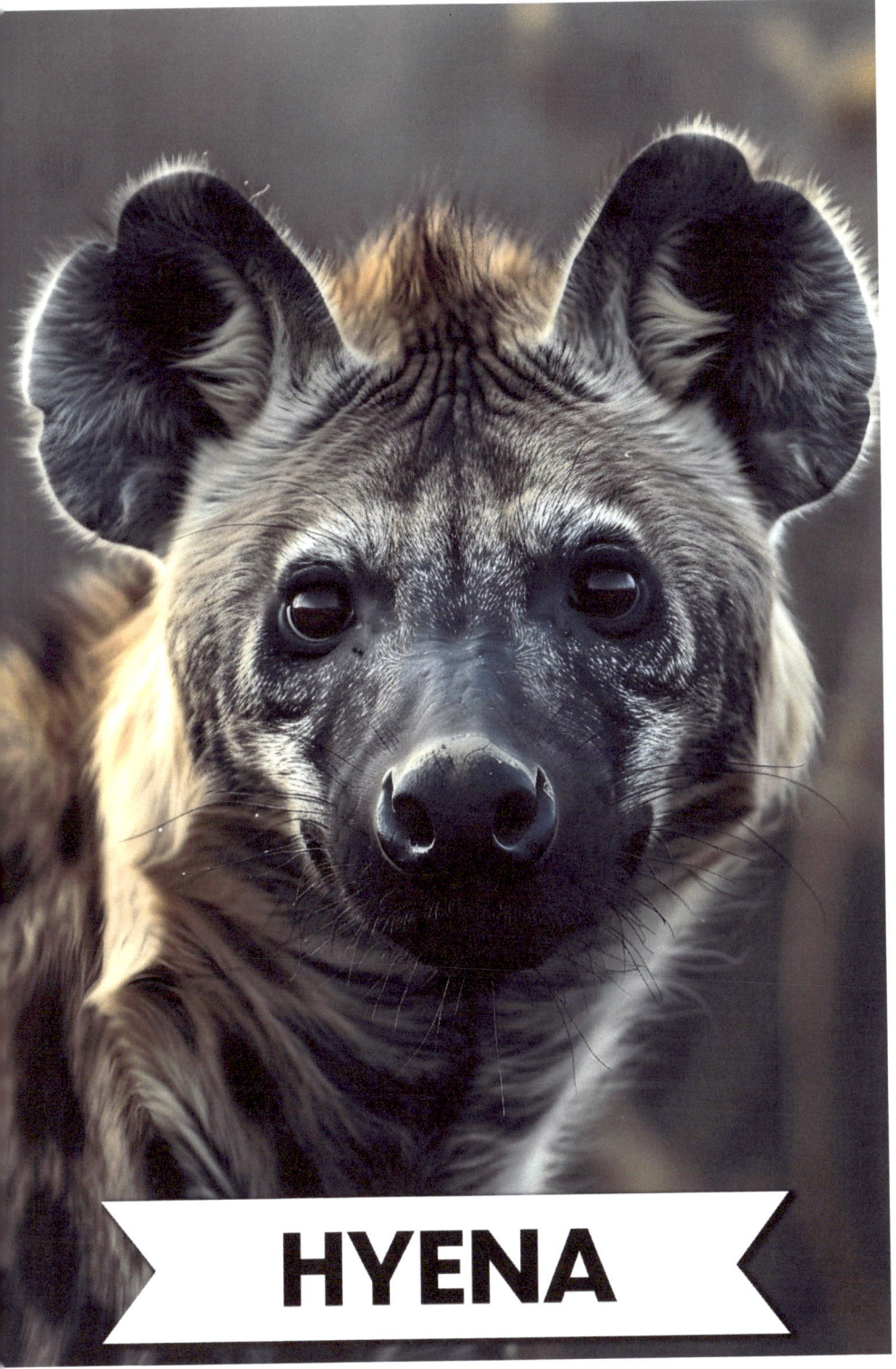

HYENA

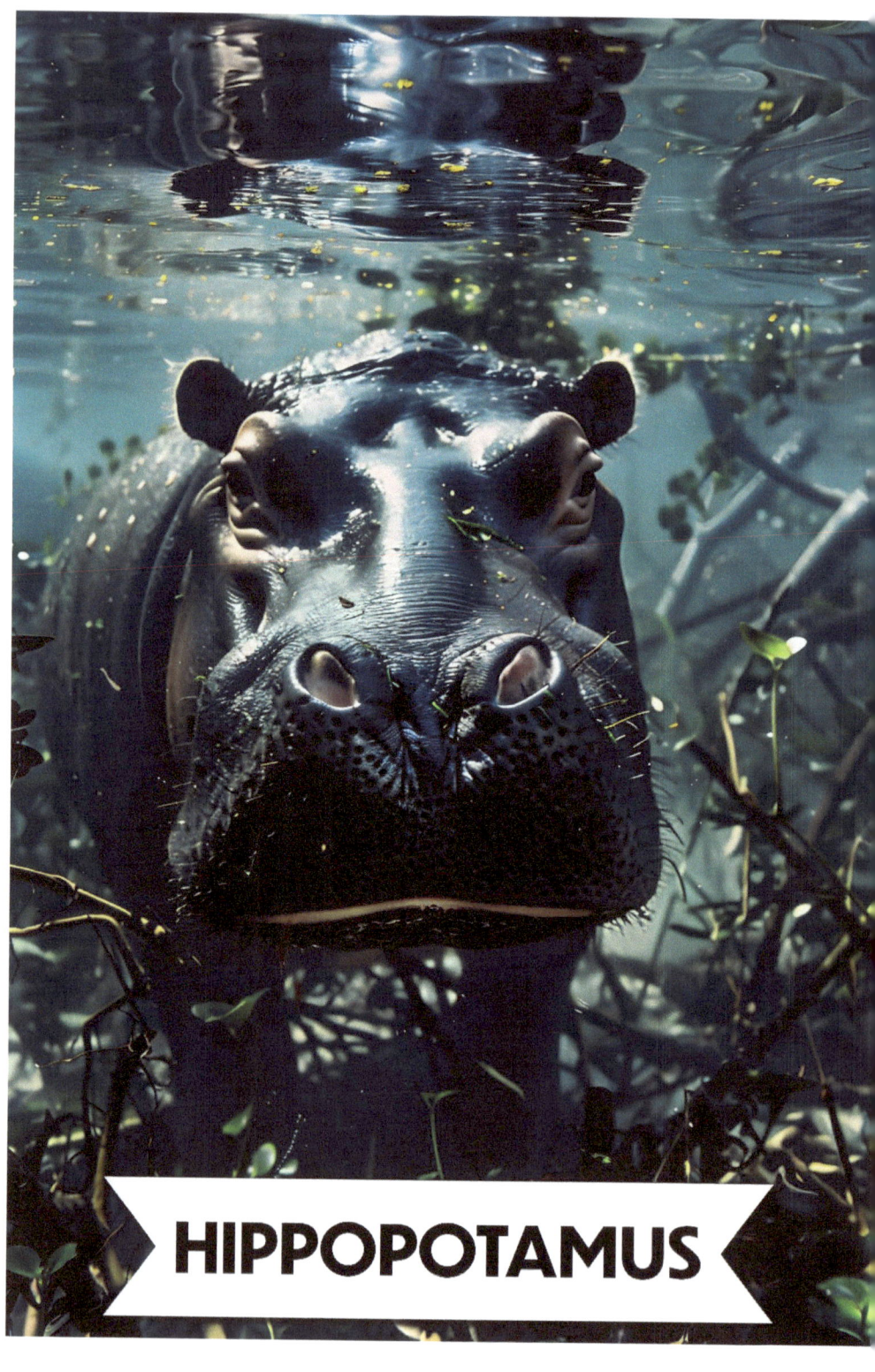

HIPPOPOTAMUS

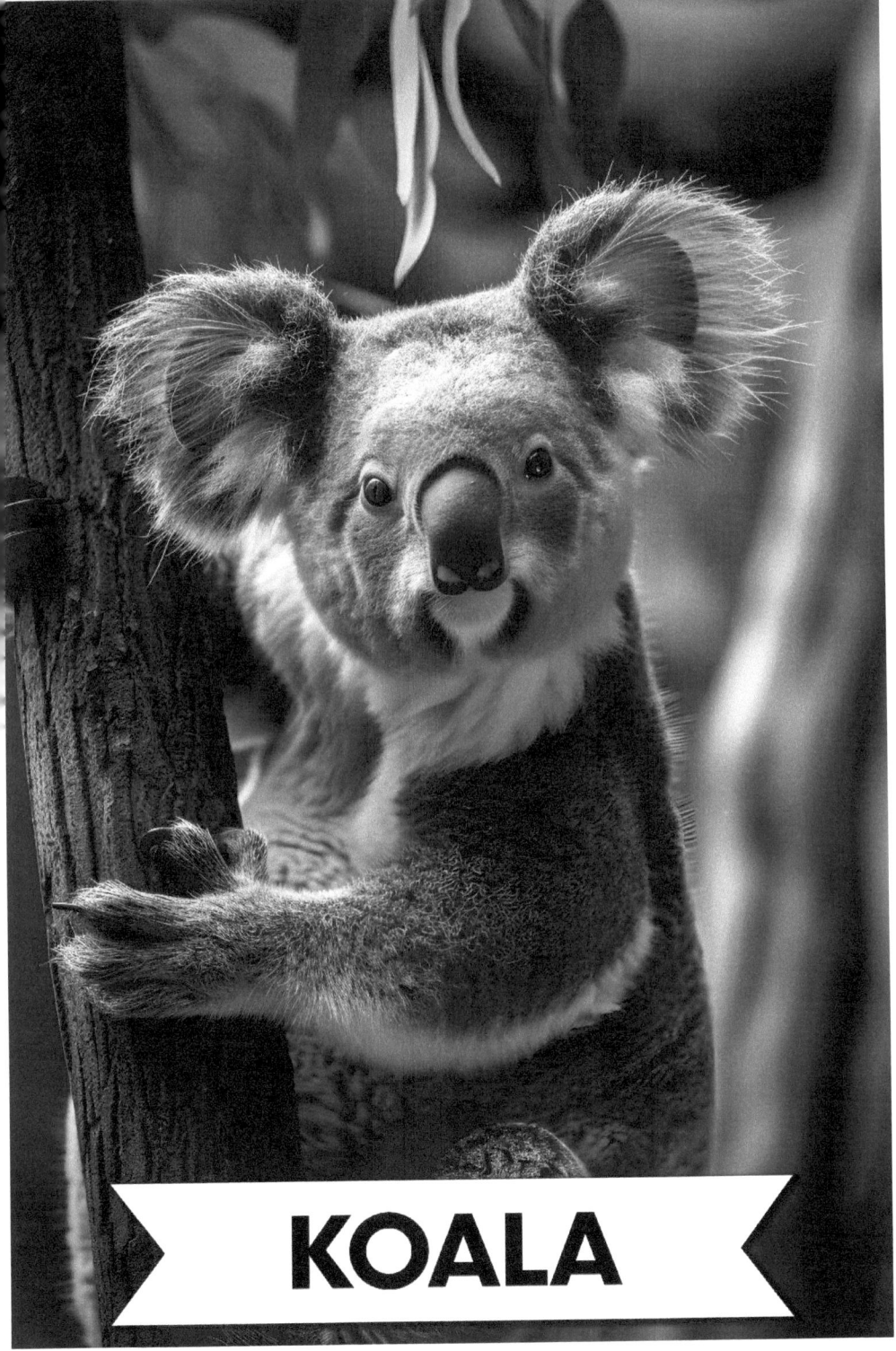

KOALA

KANGAROO

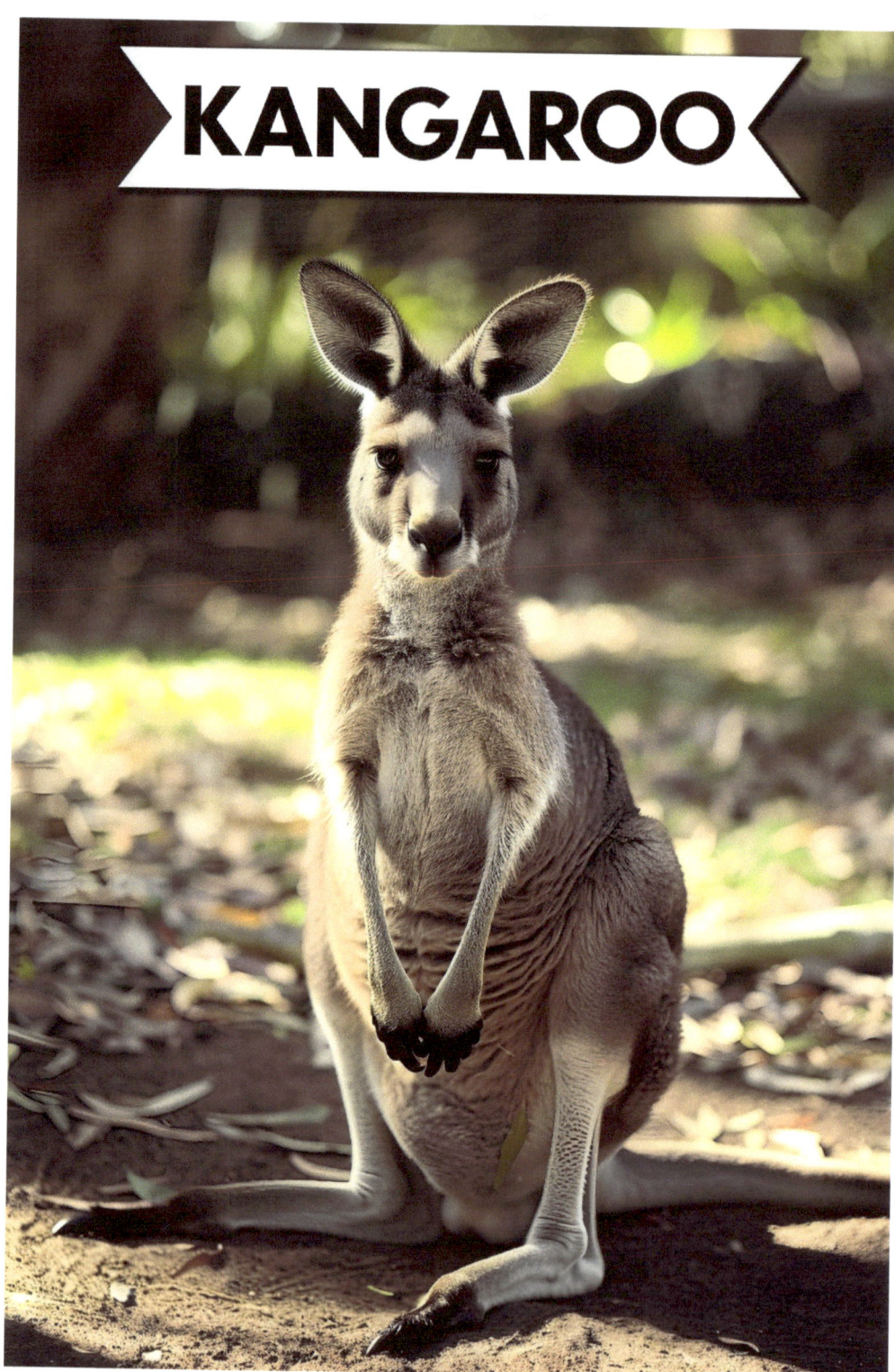

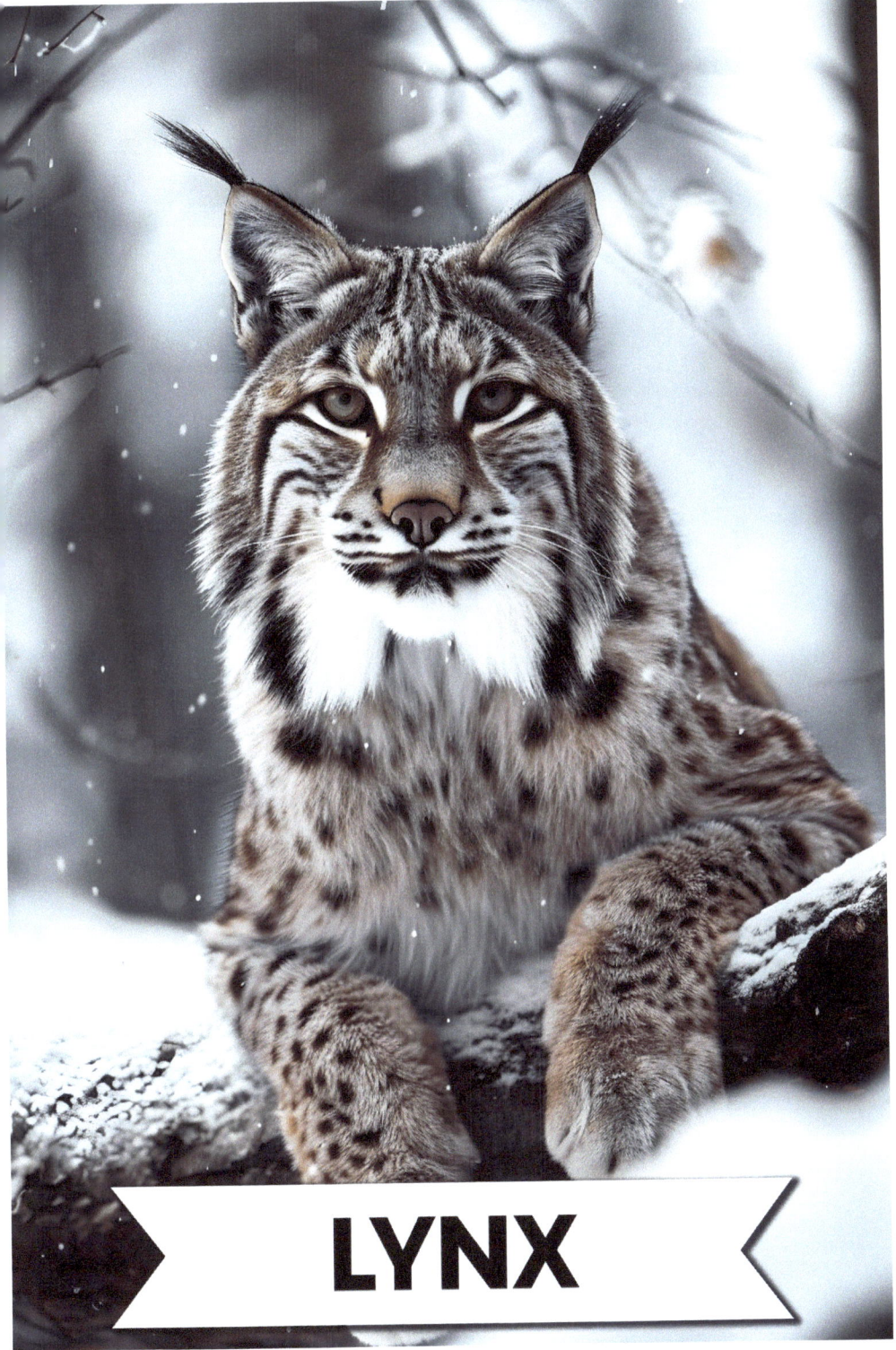

LYNX

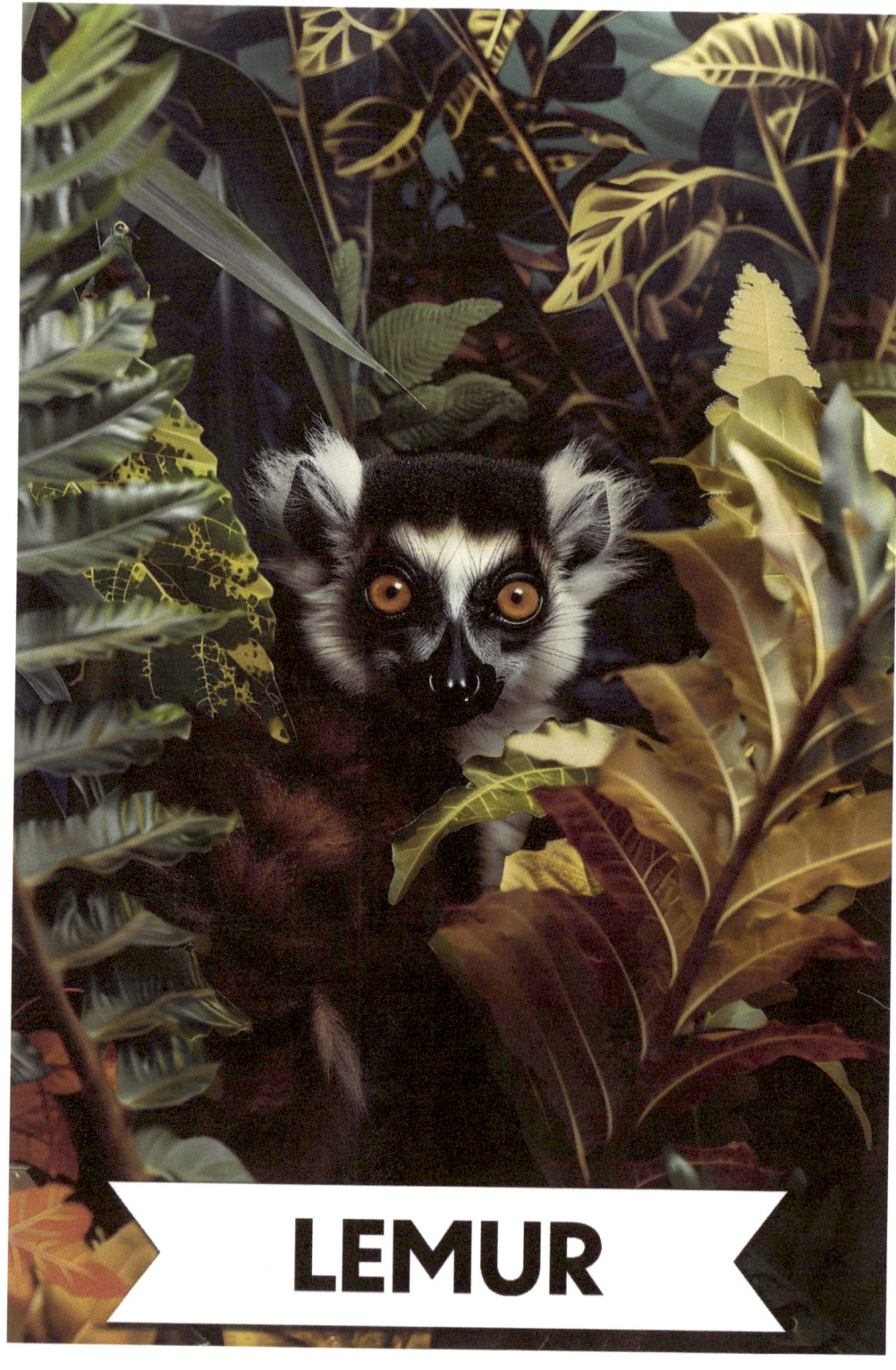

LEMUR

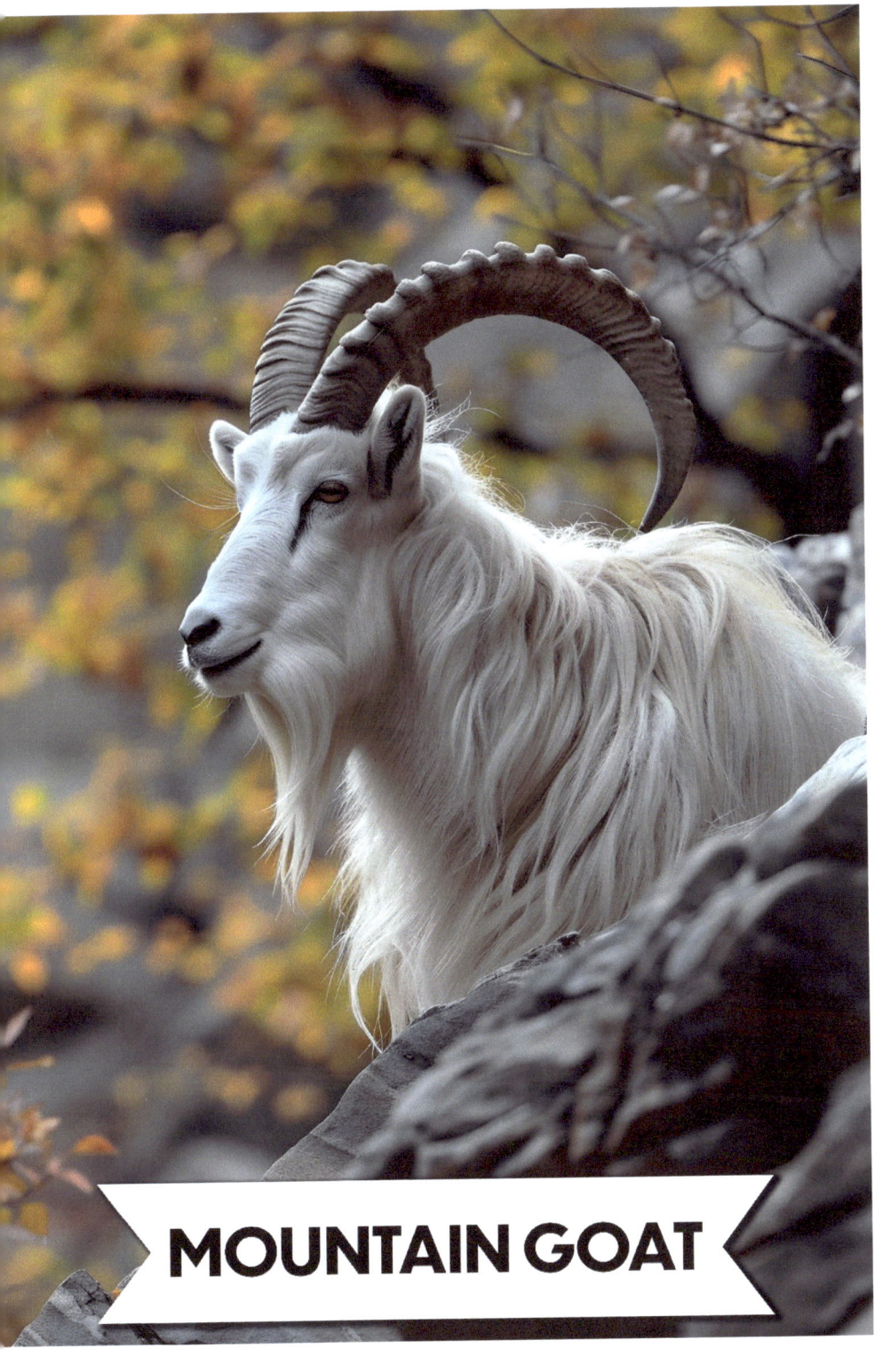

MOUNTAIN GOAT

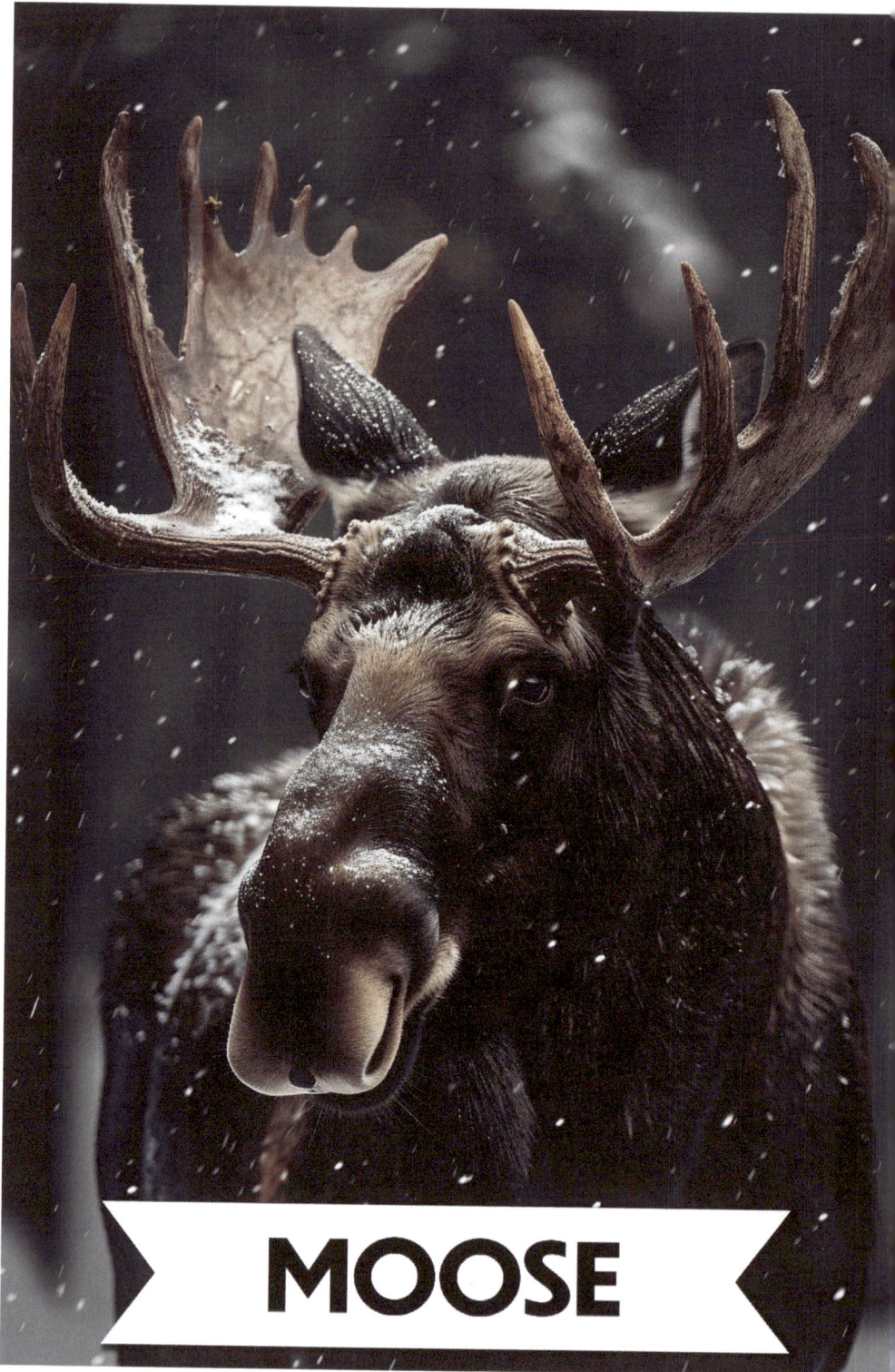

MOOSE

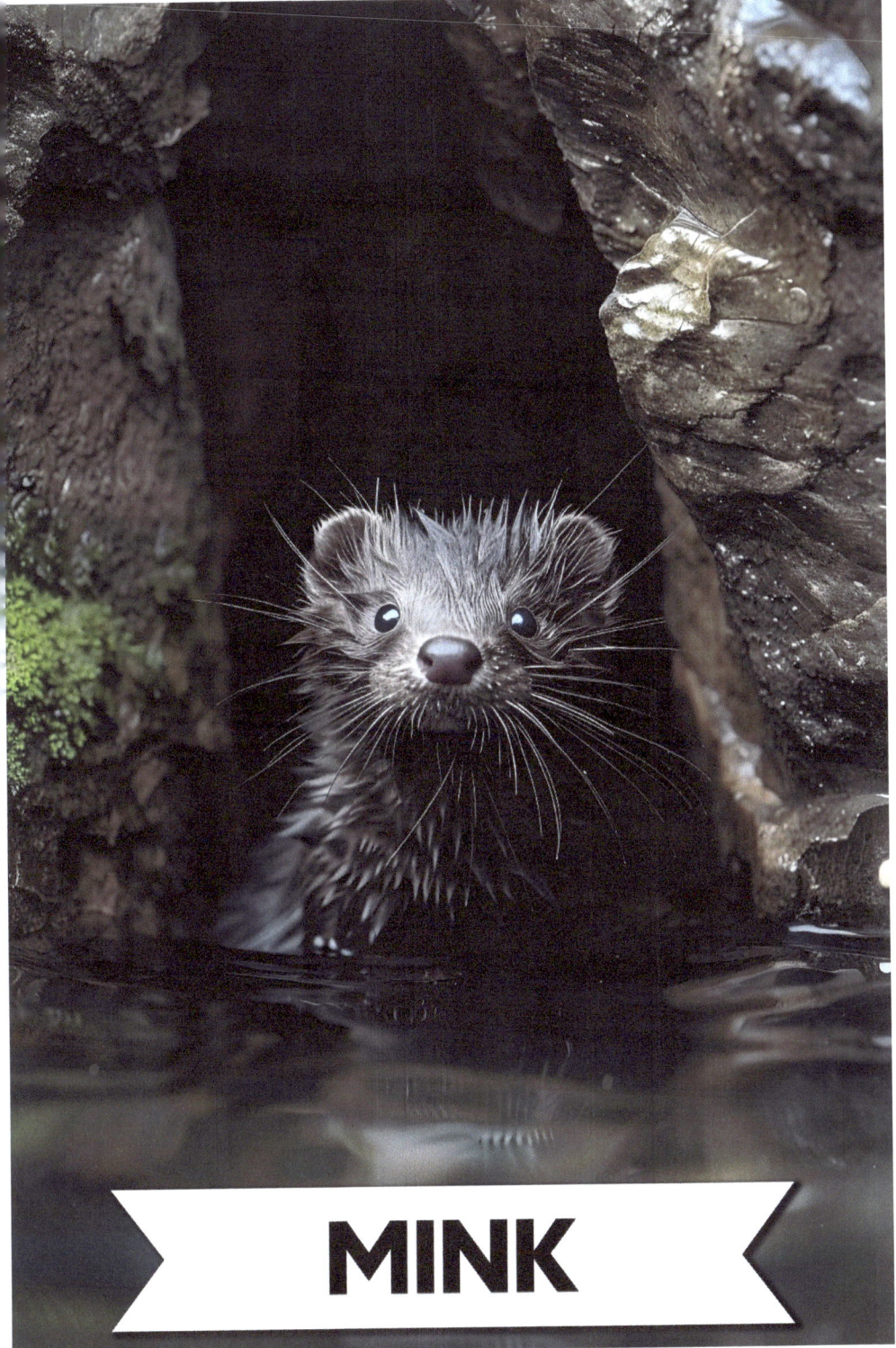

MINK

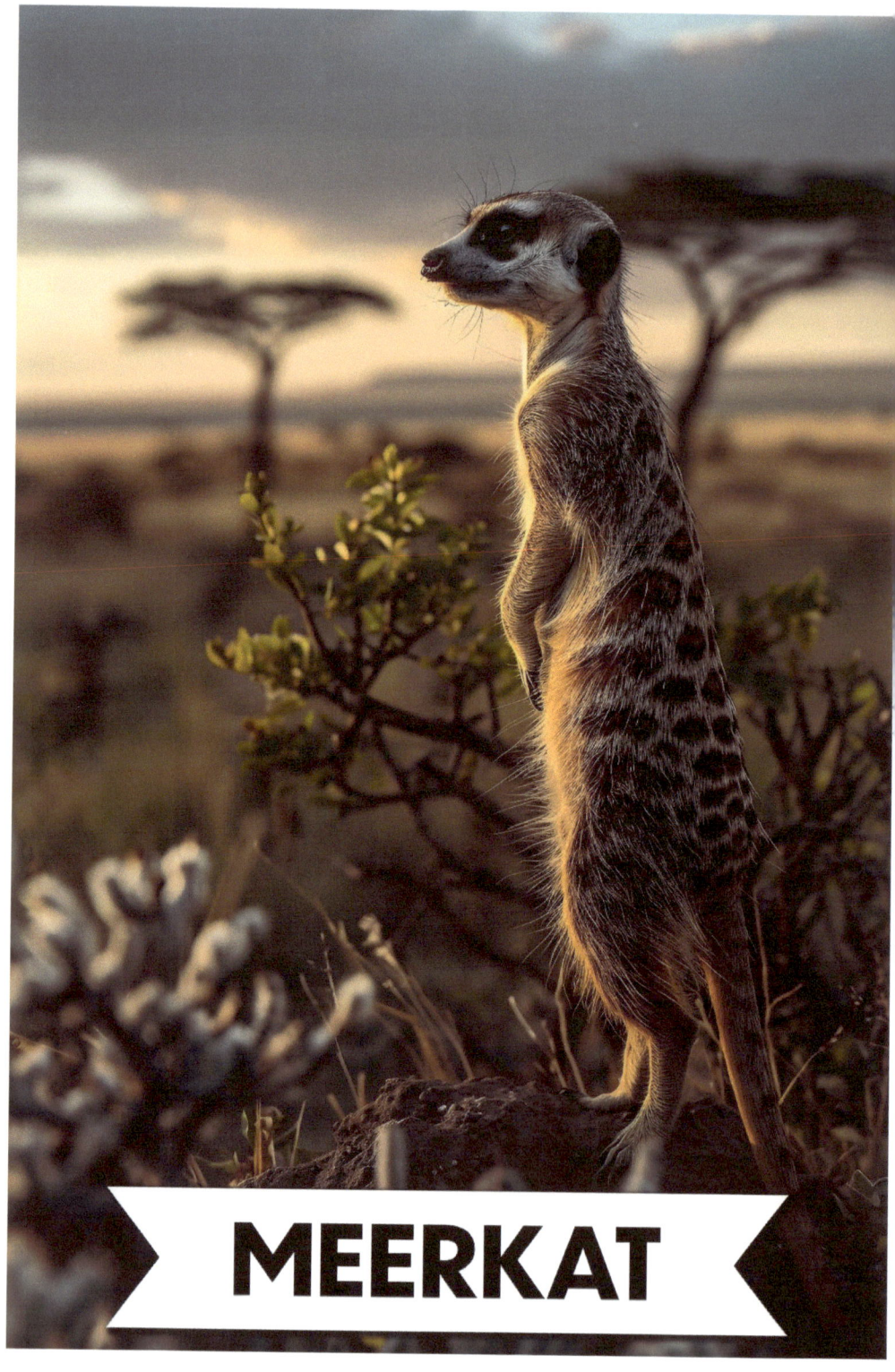

MEERKAT

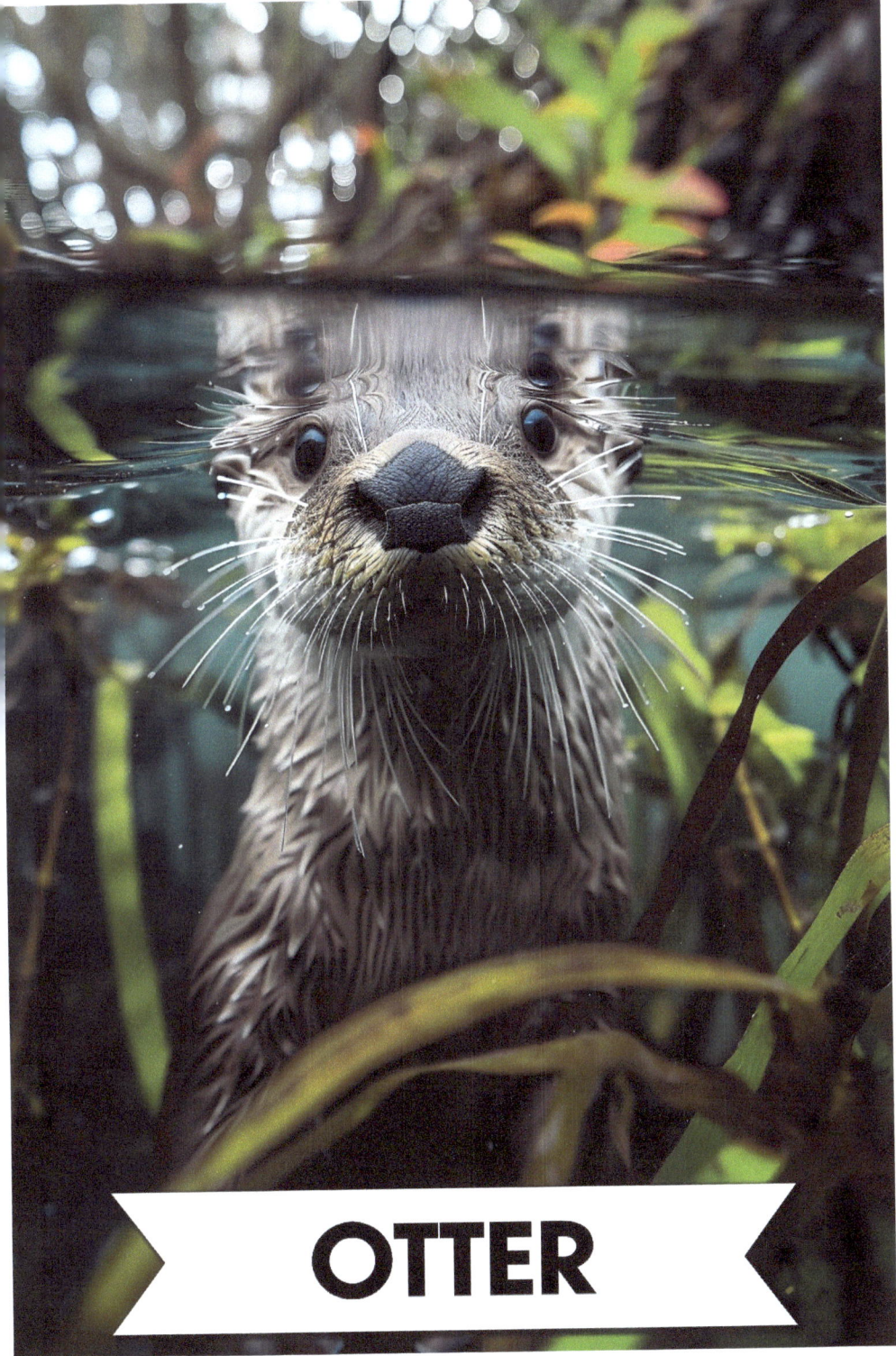

OTTER

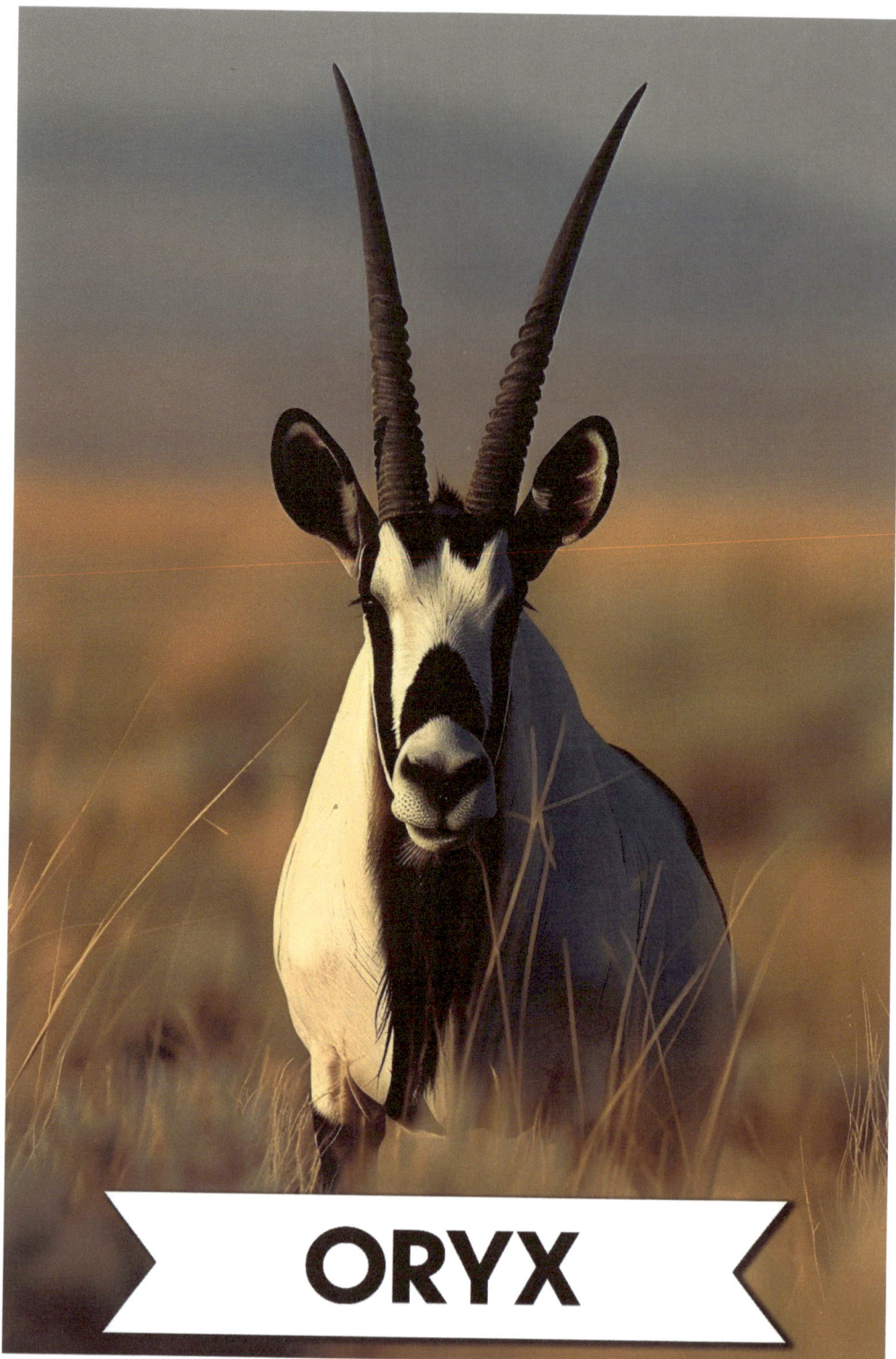

ORYX

PANDA

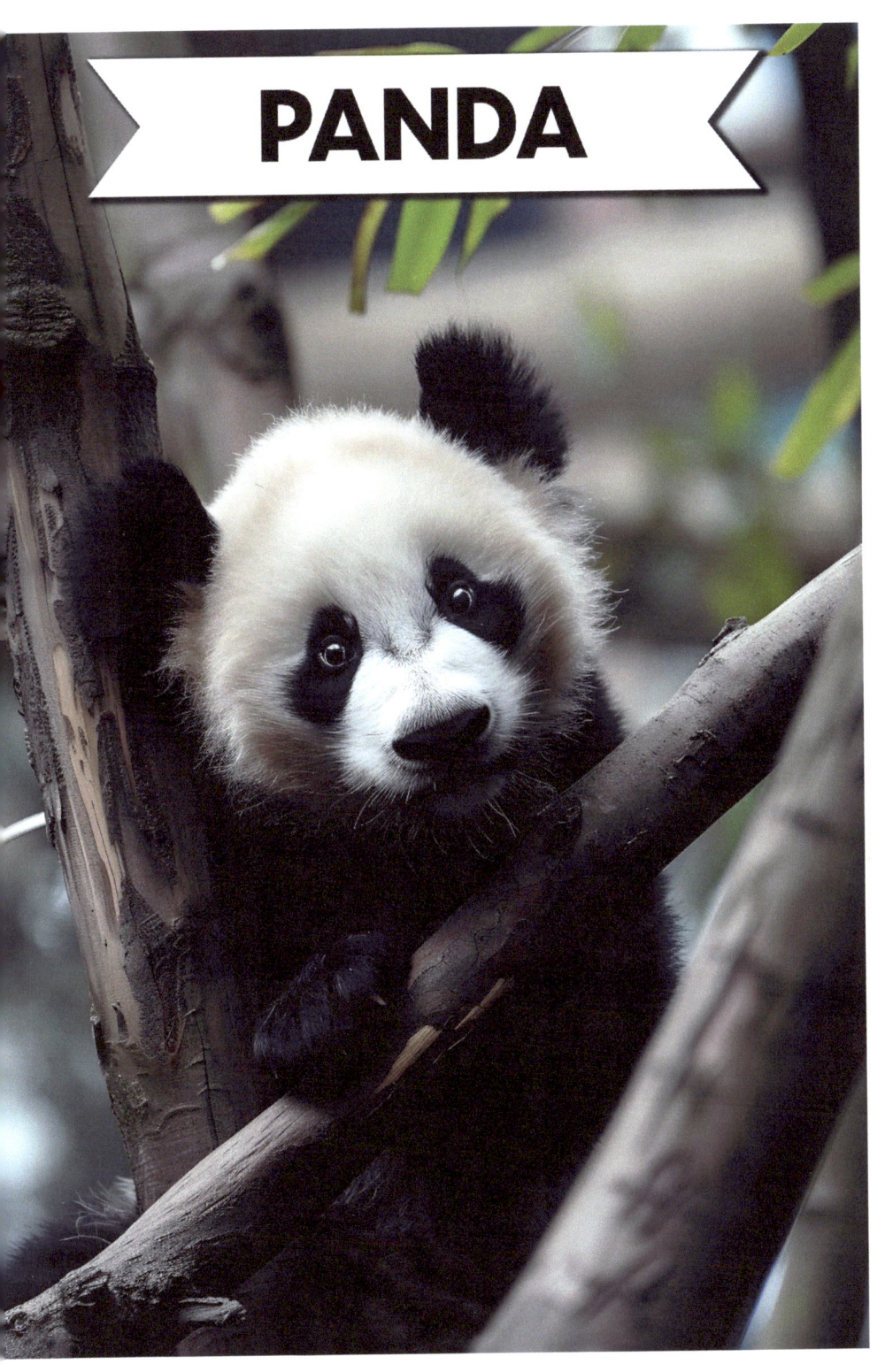

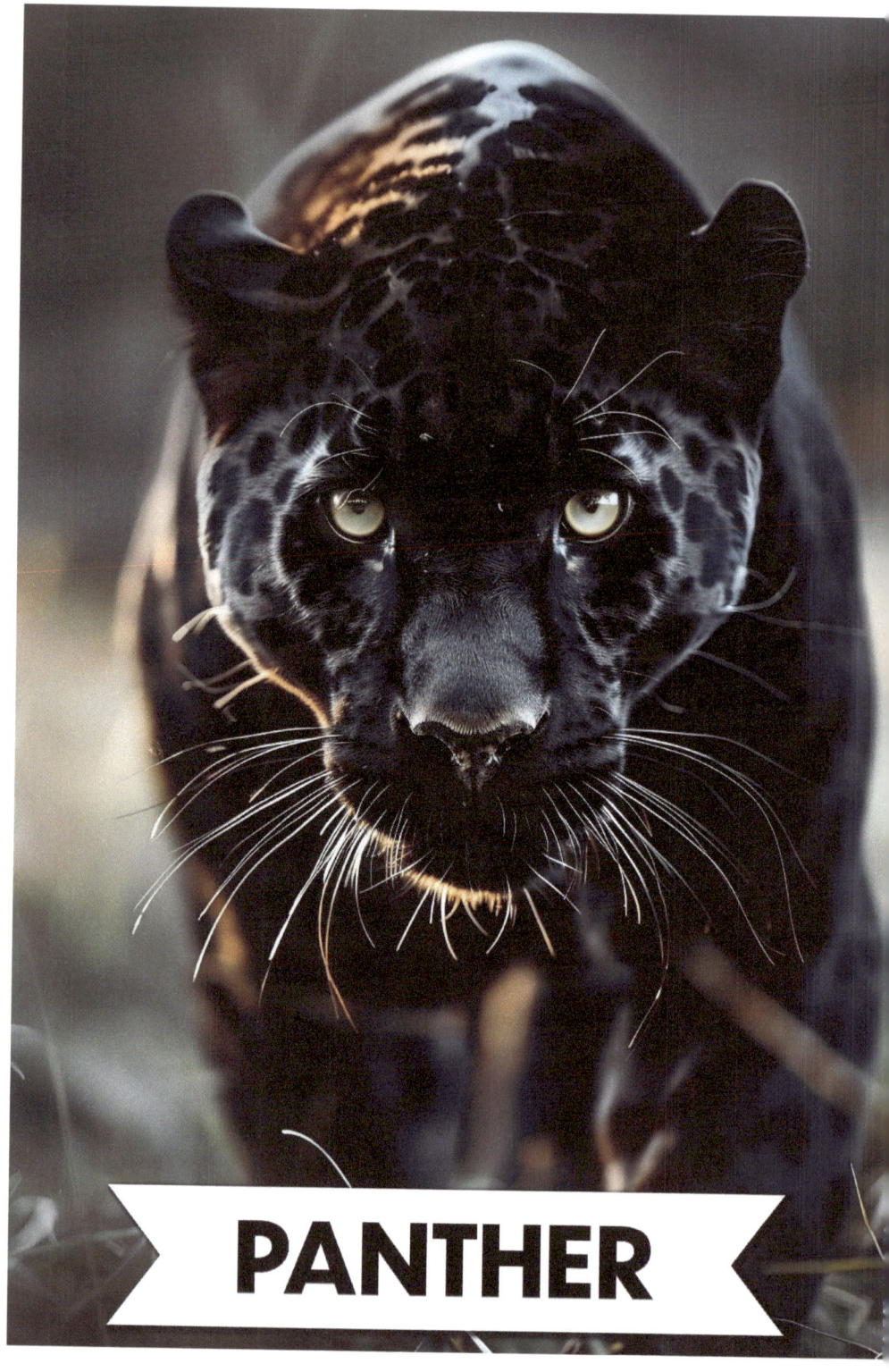

PANTHER

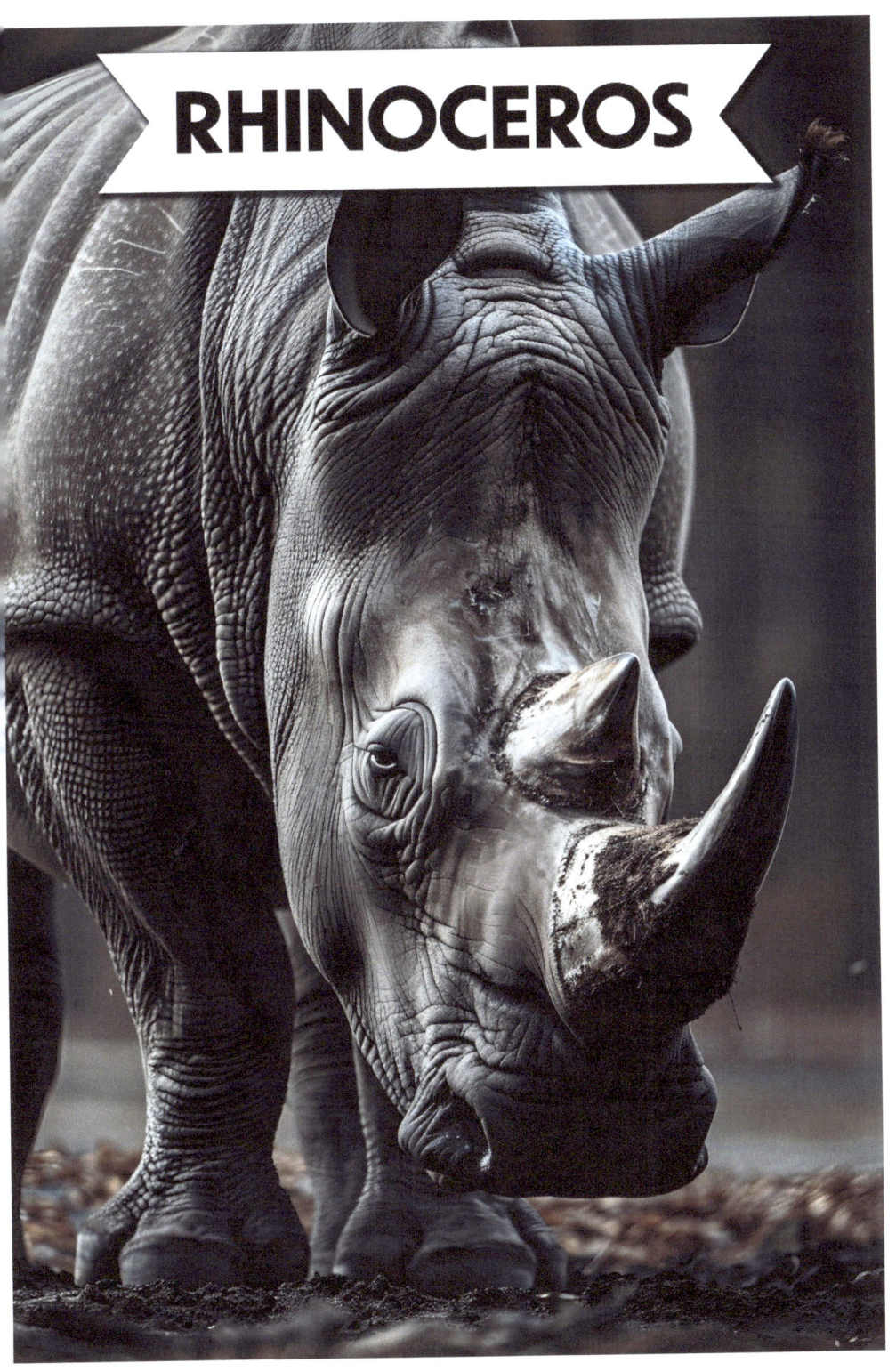

RHINOCEROS

RED PANDA

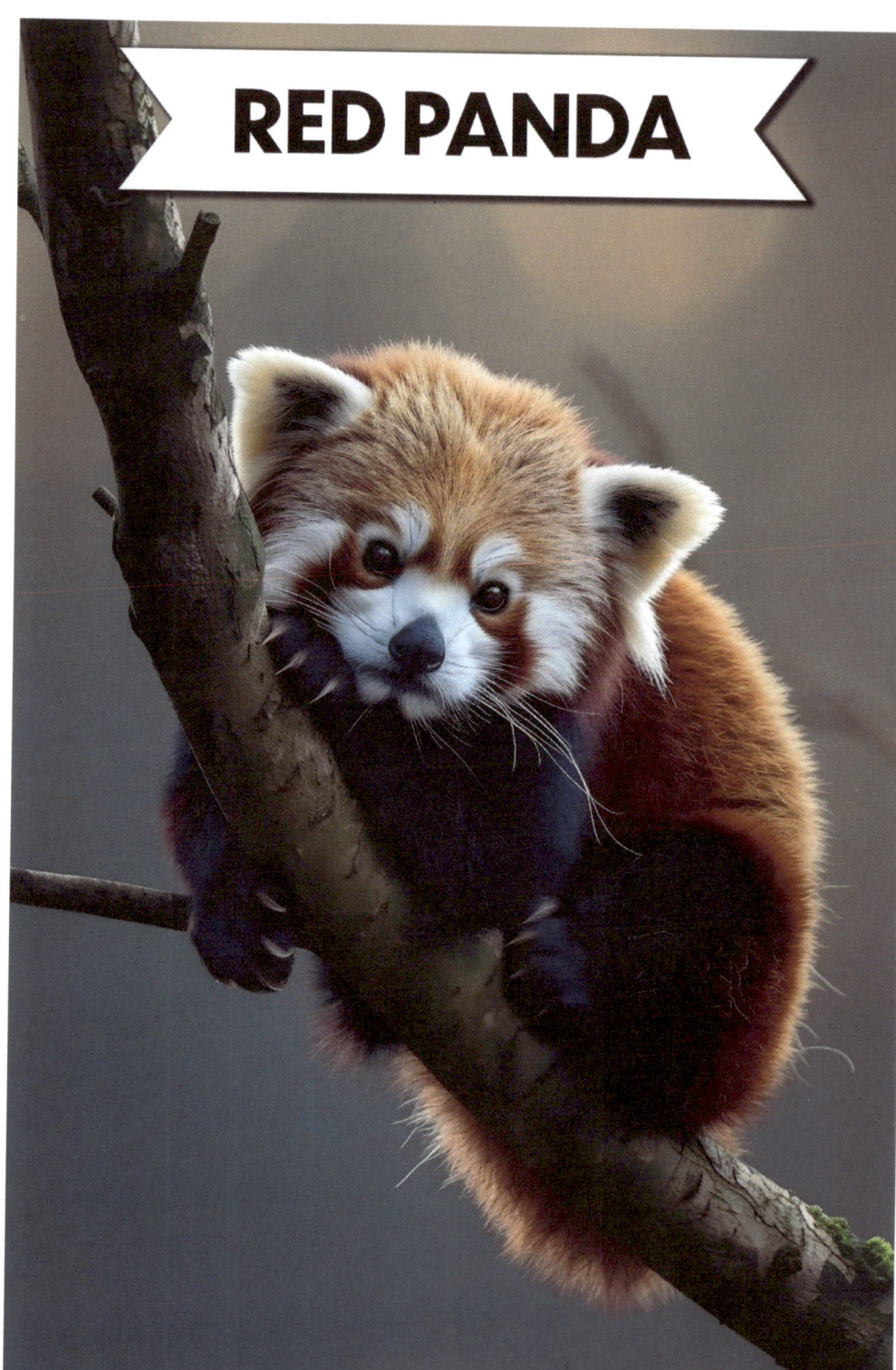

RACCOON

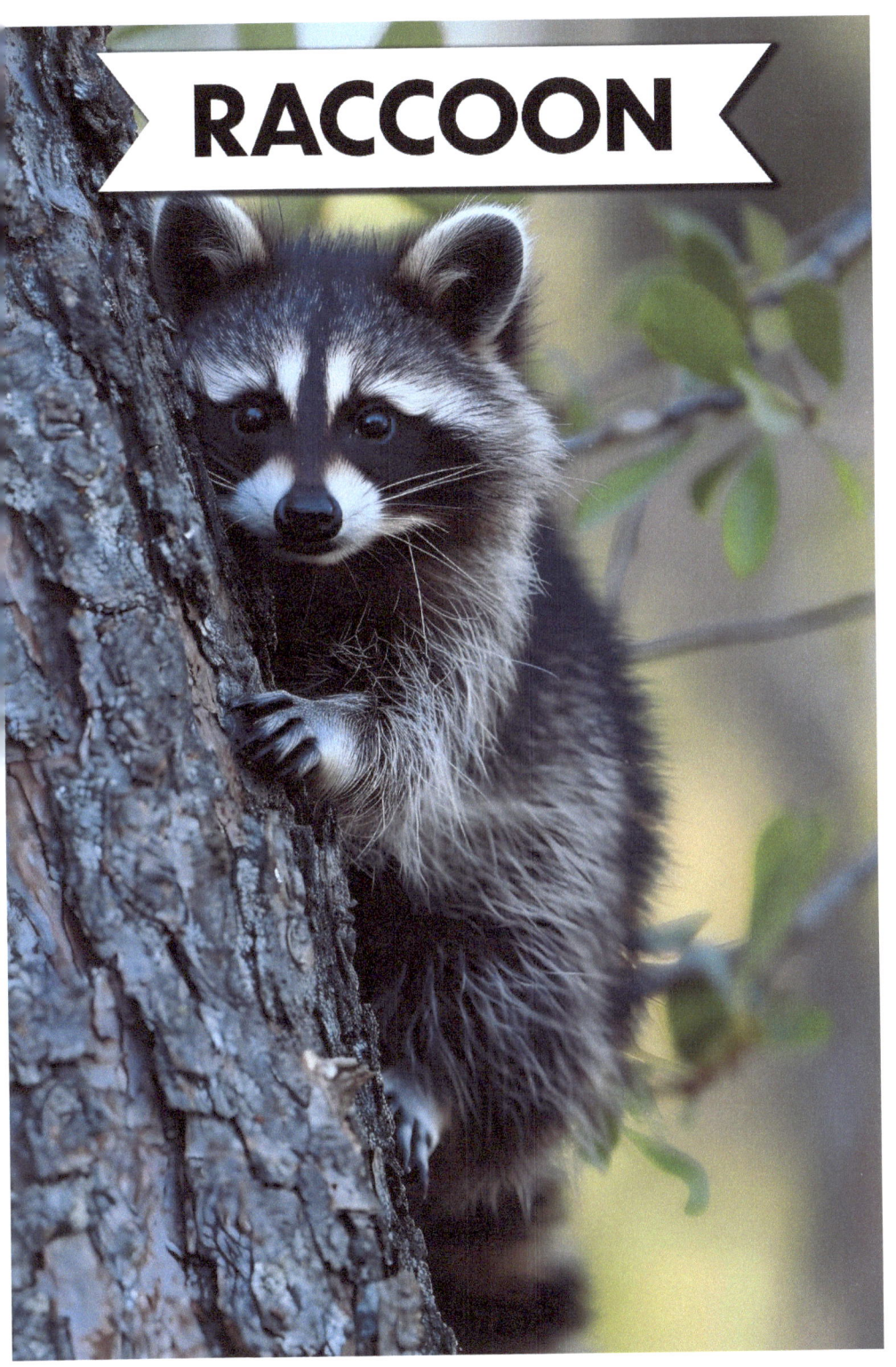

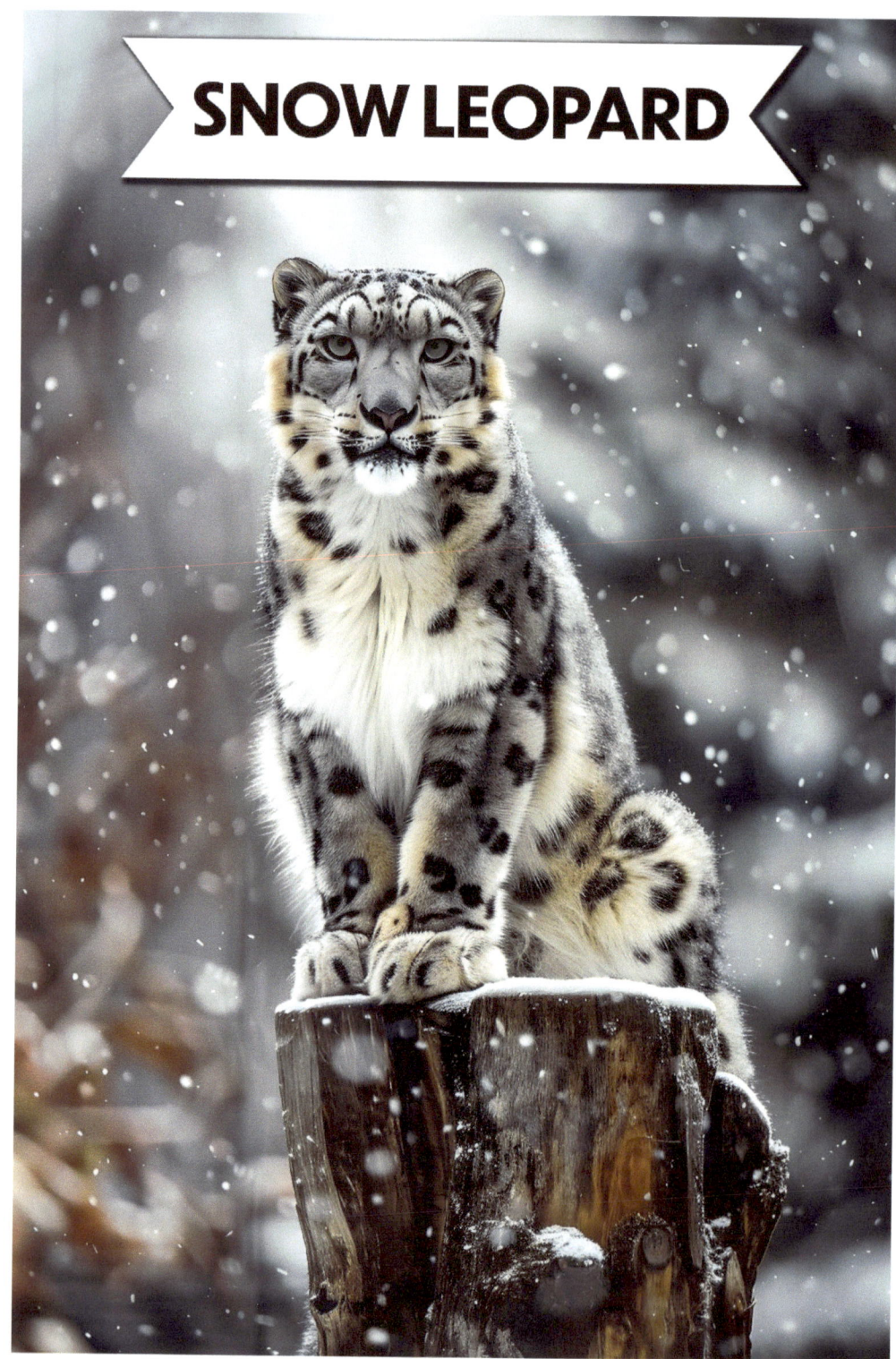

SNOW LEOPARD

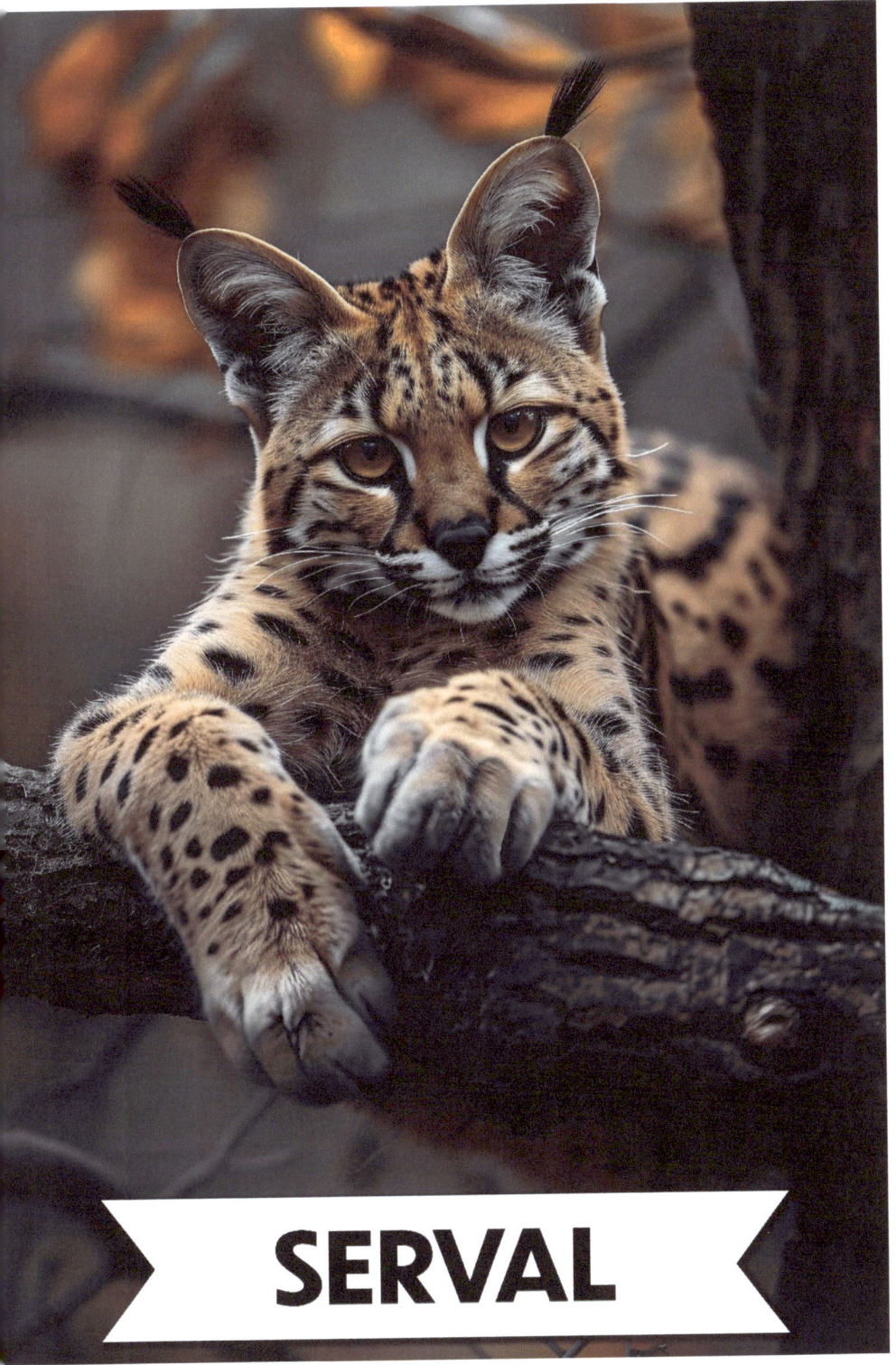

SERVAL

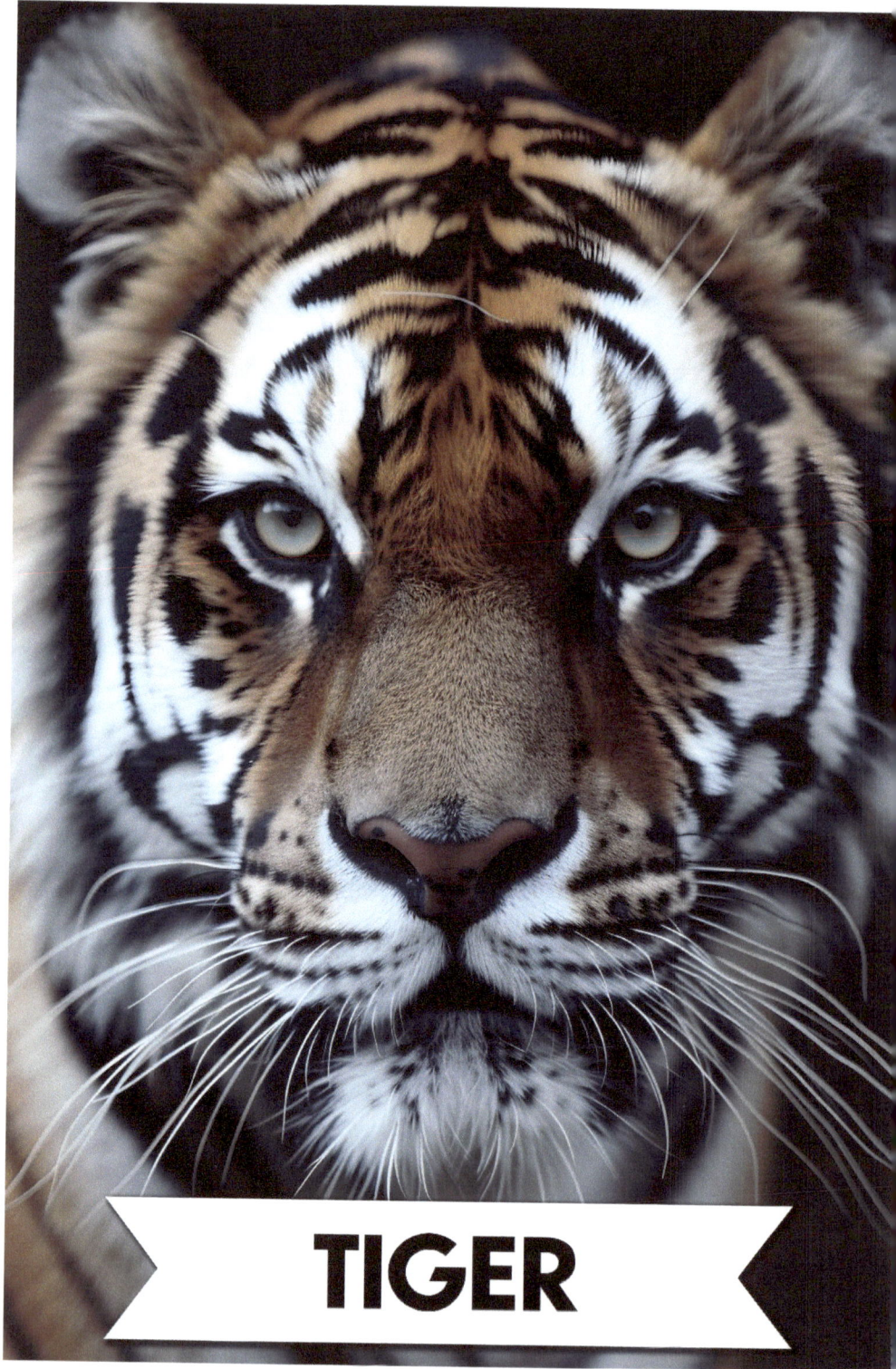

TIGER

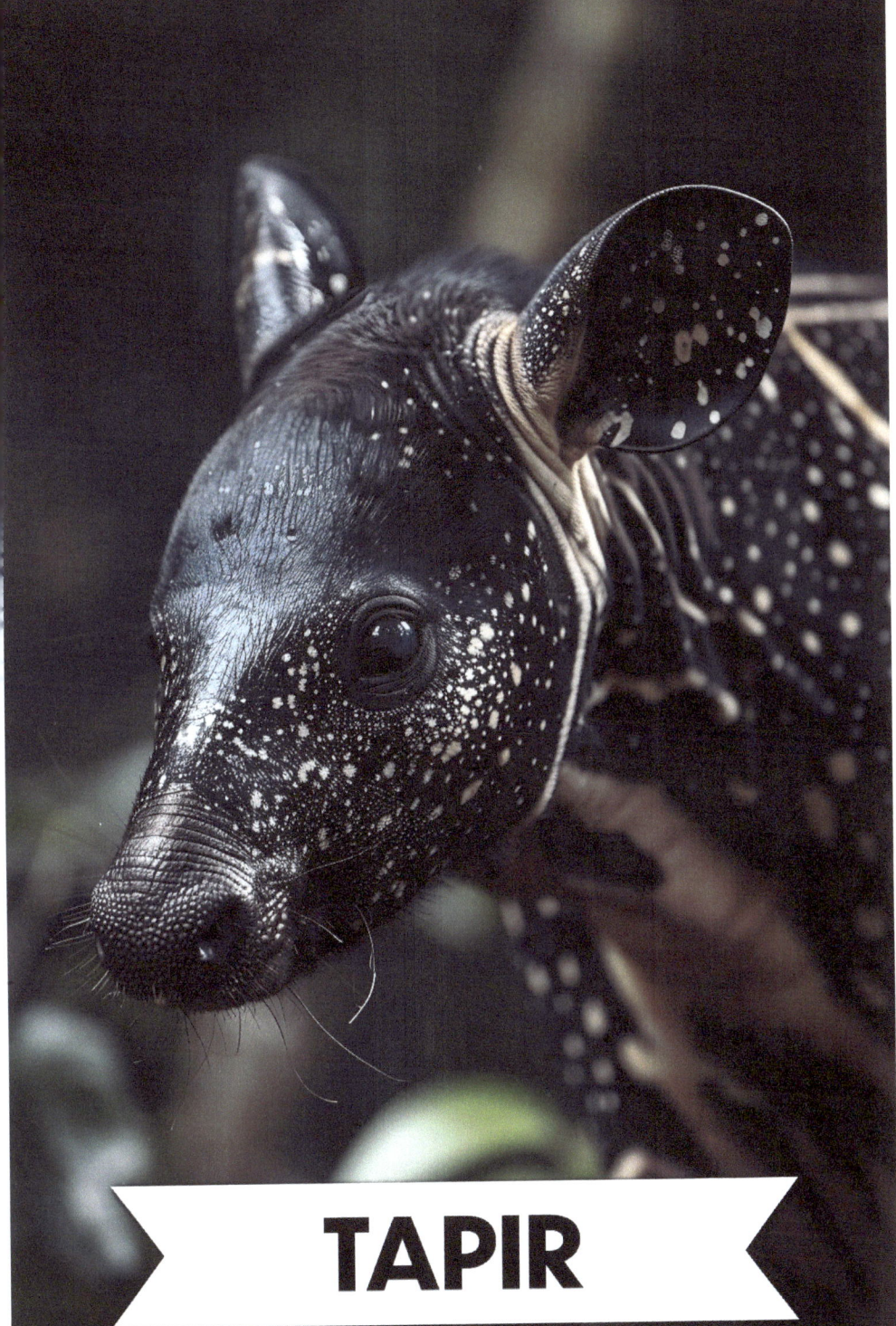

TAPIR

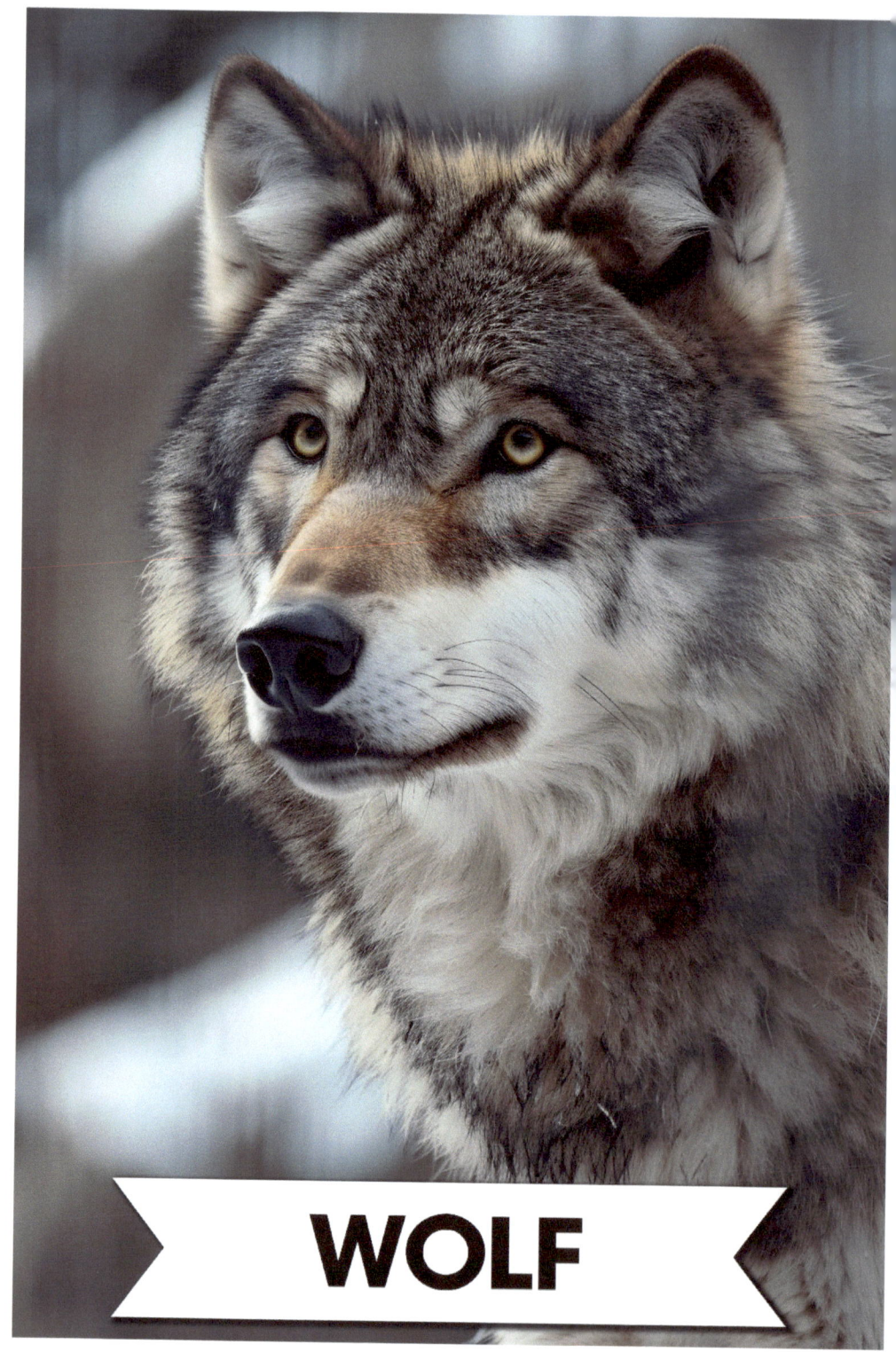

WOLF

WILDEBEEST

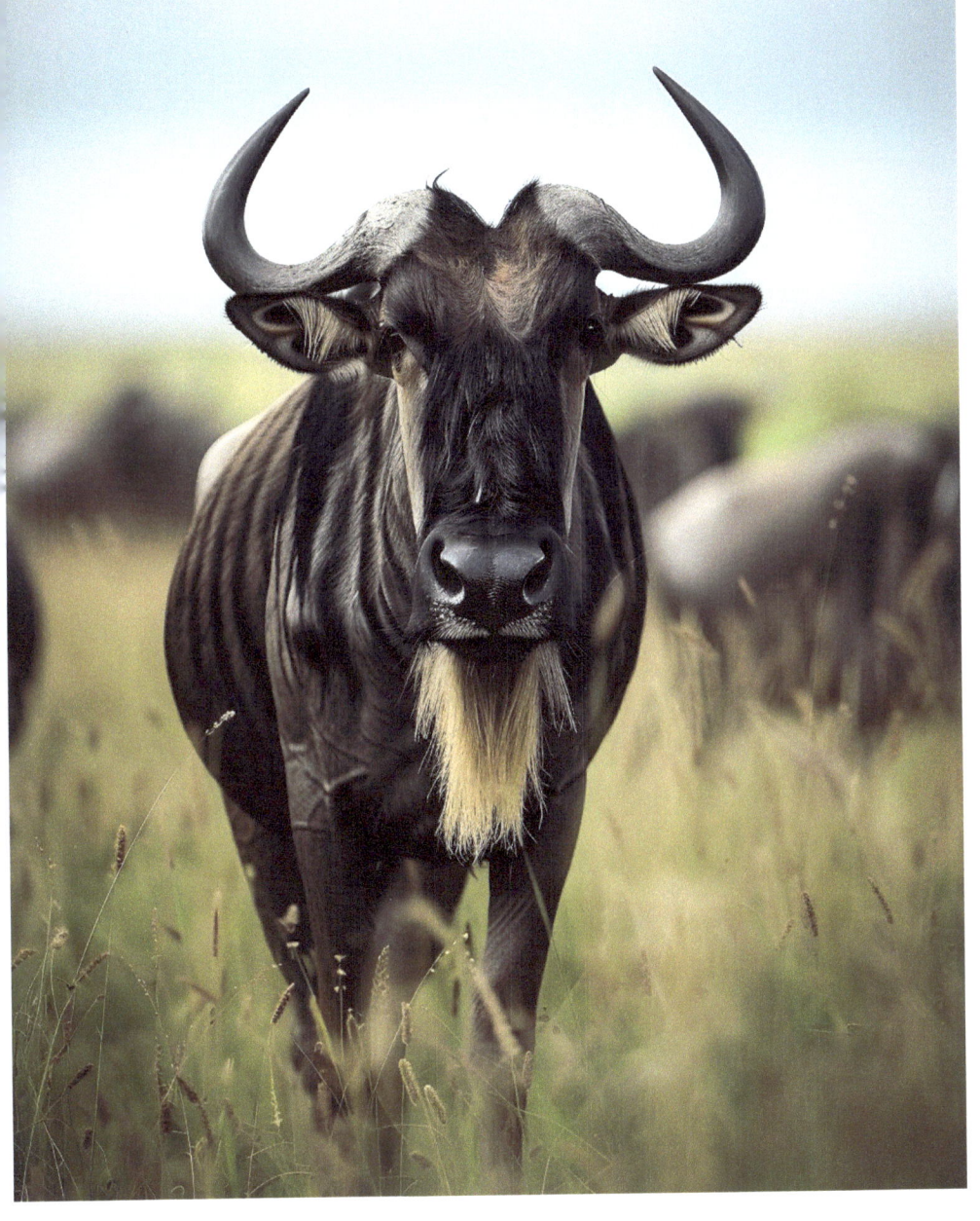

WALLABY

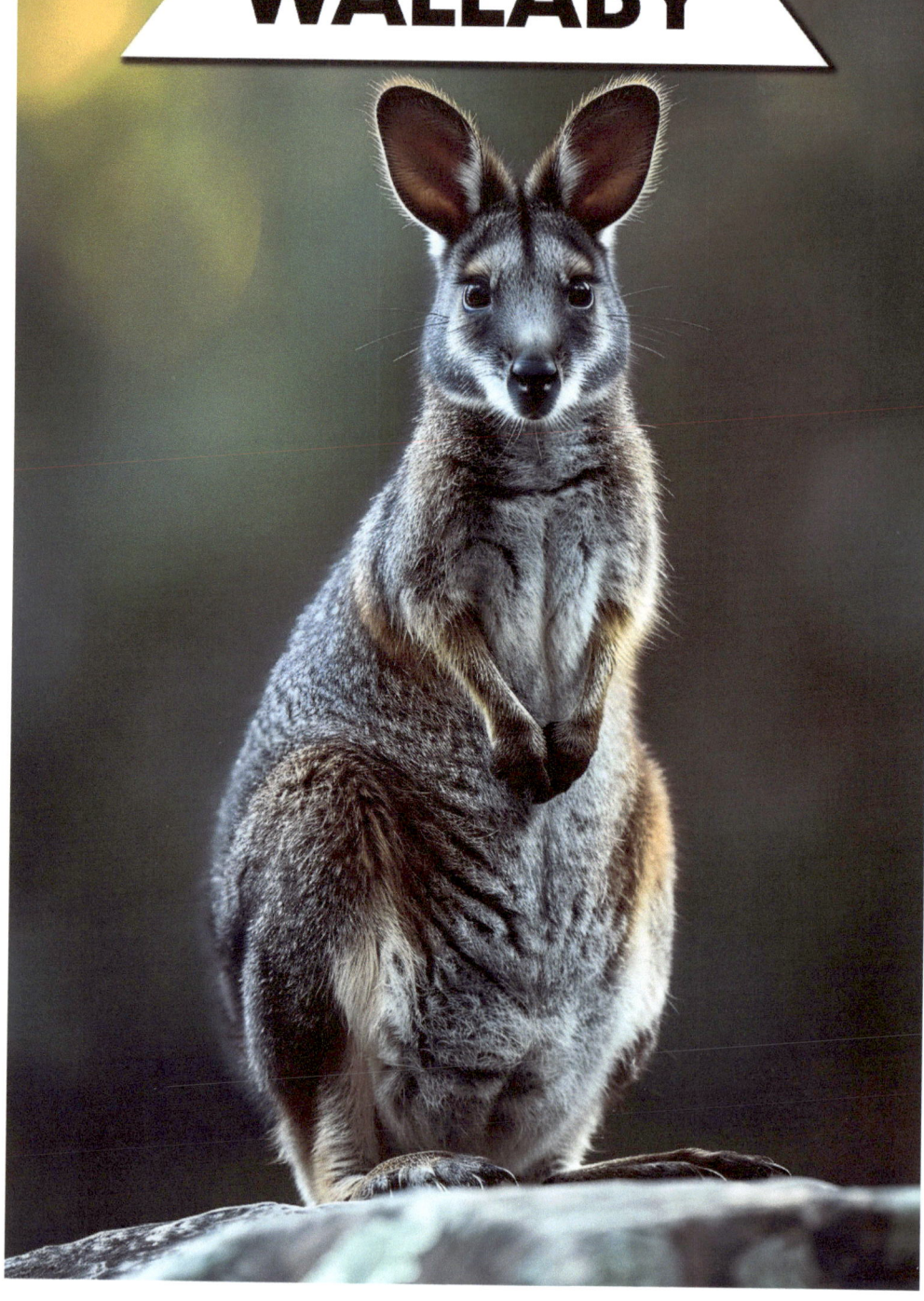

www.ingramcontent.com/pod-product-compliance
Lightning Source LLC
Chambersburg PA
CBHW040759240526
45474CB00008B/119